EASY HISTORY FOR KIDS: THE AMERICAN REVOLUTION

THE YOUNG READERS' FUN AND INTERESTING GUIDE TO EARLY AMERICAN HISTORY

☆ ☆ ☆ ☆ ☆ ☆ ☆ ☆ ☆ ☆ ☆ ☆ ☆

CURIOSITY CLASS PUBLISHING

CONTENTS

THE BEGINNING OF THE STORY

The history of our country began a long time ago. Back then, it wasn't called the United States and wasn't as big as it is now. It took many years and lots of effort to build up our country.

The Declaration of Independence was the moment when the United States became a free country. That's the moment when our history begins. However, it didn't happen in one night!

Around 400 years ago, Native people lived in these lands. One day, ships coming from Europe arrived on the east coast. Where did they come from? What did they want? Who were these people who built a new nation?

THE TIME WHEN THE EUROPEANS CAME TO AMERICA

Why did the Europeans come to America in the first place? They lived far away, crossing the ocean and settling in uncharted lands. They learned to live in a place they didn't know. In fact, they weren't even looking for a new place to live, but let's see what happened!

Everything began when an Italian sailor called Cristopher Columbus sailed west towards India in Southeast Asia. He wanted to prove that the earth was round and find a new trading route.

The Spanish monarchs had entrusted him with a mission: To find a new way to reach the Asian coasts. They used to travel through the Mediterranean Sea, but the Ottoman Empire had taken control of the region. The European kingdoms had their commercial activities interrupted.

That's why the Spanish Queen Isabella gave Columbus three ships to embark on a great adventure. He was traveling through uncharted waters. Nobody had ventured to cross the Atlantic Ocean before. However, instead of Asia, he landed on a little island in the middle of the Caribbean Sea. Today, that island belongs to the Bahamas.

At first, he didn't know it was a brand-new continent. He thought he had accomplished his mission. Although, he was right, and by sailing west, he would have reached India eventually. There was no way for him to know that he would come across another continent while making his journey.

On October 12th, 1492, Columbus and part of his crew finally landed in what he thought was India. That's why he called the Native people "Indians." Soon, Columbus learned that those lands were filled with treasures: Gold, silver, gems, and many goods that Europeans didn't even know existed, such as chocolate and corn.

He returned to Europe to tell the Spanish king and queen about everything he had discovered. Shortly after, every king in Europe also wanted the wealth of these beautiful lands. Then, many excursions came from Europe to what was called the

"New World," searching for metals, goods, and more lands for their empires.

It took a while before the Europeans realized it wasn't India or Asia but a whole new continent. Many years later, the continent appeared on the maps with the name "America."

THE TIME WHEN THE FIRST CONQUERORS ARRIVED IN NORTH AMERICA

At the end of the 1700s, the Spanish, Dutch, French, and British explored the shores of North America. The Spanish and the French settled in the south, which is known today as Florida. However, it wasn't easy for all the Europeans to establish colonies as the Spanish and Portuguese had in the rest of the continent.

The French succeeded in settling in the margins of the St. Lawrence River and the Great Lakes region. The Spanish took control of the lands in the south of North America. The British monarchy also had interests in America. At first, the monarchs sent privateers (more about these later) to sail the Caribbean Sea and capture Spanish vessels full of metals. Then, Sir Walter Raleigh settled the first British colony in North America. It was placed on Roanoke Island, off North Carolina. However, the small population didn't last; within a couple of years, it disappeared.

THE FIRST BRITISH COLONY

Queen Elizabeth I sponsored sailors known as privateers, a type of pirate where the booty was stolen for the queen.

THE BEGINNING OF THE STORY

John Hawkins and Francis Drake were commissioned to hunt and steal from Spanish vessels.

Some years later, after the disappearance of Roanoke Island, ships of the London Company arrived in Chesapeake Bay in April 1607. People on the ships didn't know they were about to become the first permanent English settlers in the New World. There were 105 men: 40 were soldiers, 35 were nobles, and the rest were artisans and laborers. In Europe, people heard about the charms of the new continent, and many wanted to come. Some just wanted a fantastic adventure, and others wanted to make themselves rich.

That first colony was called Jamestown to honor the King of England, James I. He had given an order to the London Company to explore these lands. Later, when the colony expanded, it was called Virginia. It was the first of 13 colonies founded by the British in North America, on the east coast by the Atlantic Ocean. The 13 colonies were divided into three regions: New England, Middle Colonies, and Southern Colonies.

It took the British almost a hundred years to create the 13 colonies. Each of the colonies was founded for a particular purpose. For instance, Jamestown was a port whose main purpose was trade.

Life wasn't easy for the settlers. They had to face a lot of dangers: Attacks from the local populations who didn't want them there, assaults from the other nations' armies that wanted to conquer more lands, illnesses, and money issues. It wasn't as easy to flourish in the New World as they believed it would before embarking on the adventure.

CHAPTER 1
SETTING THE SCENE

The British monarch realized that the other kings of Europe were expanding their empires. That wasn't good for Great Britain. In those times, monarchies were constantly competing with each other, and more lands and resources meant that the British enemies were stronger. Therefore, the British doubled their efforts to bring more settlers to America and establish more British and, eventually, royal colonies:

1. **Virginia, established** in 1607, became a royal colony in 1624
2. **New York**, established in 1664, became a royal colony in 1685
3. **Massachusetts** was established in 1620 and became royal in 1691
4. **Maryland**, established in 1632, was declared a royal colony in 1692.
5. **Rhode Island**, established in 1636, received its royal charter in 1663

6. **Connecticut**, established in 1636, became a royal colony in 1662

7. **New Hampshire**, established in 1623, became a royal colony in 1679

8. **Delaware**, established in 1664, became a royal colony in 1707

9. **North Carolina**, established in 1663, became a royal colony in 1729

10. South Carolina, established in 1663, became a royal colony in 1729

11. **New Jersey**, established in 1664, became a royal colony in 1702

12. **Pennsylvania**, established in 1681, became a royal colony in 1707

13. **Georgia**, established in 1732, became a royal colony in 1752

Some of the colonies resulted from the British king's efforts to expand his influence on America and compete with the other kingdoms. The economic situation in England was complicated, and the King thought the lands in America could provide new job opportunities for people. There, people could have their own land to farm and produce what they needed to survive.

Some of the colonies were born from the initiative of the settlers. It was the time of the Protestant Reformation in Europe, and in England, it caused a lot of unrest. So, some people left the country, searching for a new place to practice their religion peacefully. In America, some of the settlers didn't agree with the rest of the community about morals and values, so they founded new colonies.

Lots of people were ready to try their luck in America. They believed it was an opportunity to improve their living conditions. They weren't intimidated by the great challenge, as when they first arrived, there was nothing.

They had to build the houses, the roads, the harbors, the land for the crops, and start a village from scratch. In addition, they faced constant threats of attacks and illnesses they weren't prepared for. Even so, they persisted, and the colonies eventually flourished.

From the beginning, life in the colonies was characterized by hard work and organization. Even though the colonies were under British rule, they developed their own government for local issues. They weren't free to make their own rules or vote for who ruled them, but they still had assemblies where they discussed community affairs.

THE NEW WORLD: LIFE IN THE 13 COLONIES

The Endeavor of Surviving in the New World

The men who founded Jamestown weren't aware of what life in the colony would be like. Most of them were nobles who had enough money to afford the journey. The Virginia Company brought them to America after the request of King James I, but it was each settler's decision, and people had to pay for their expenses.

Once in America, the men landed and opened a sealed box left by the Company with the instructions on how to proceed. They first had to set up a camp, so they searched for a better place further away from the coast for better protection, as The Spanish army could assault them at any moment.

The new settlers who had come to trade and start businesses in the first place didn't know about the local threats. They had camped in the lands of the Powhatan, a native population that hunted there. The British men had instructions to trade with the natives, but that wouldn't be so easy.

On top of that, the camp was surrounded by water. The settlers thought that was good because ships could easily reach the sea and come and go to Europe. What they didn't know was that those waters were infested with mosquitos, and those mosquitos transmitted malaria, a deadly disease.

Besides these troubles, they had to start a life there. When they arrived, it was too late in the year to farm. Even if they could, most people weren't peasants, who usually did the farming, so they didn't know how. The peasant settlers that were there explained to the rest that the lands were surrounded by swamps and weren't good enough for crops. Finding food was going to be another significant challenge.

The Virginia Company was concerned about the settlers. After all, they had spent a lot of money to start work in America. In the first months, the results weren't as expected. The settlers were supposed to trade with the natives, send goods to Europe, and explore to find gold, but they struggled to survive. So, they sent new ships with supplies from England to help the settlers.

Despite the initial tension, the Powhatan natives established relationships with the foreign settlers and sent them food. This helped the settlers survive while they waited for the Company's assistance.

Eventually, ships with more people and supplies arrived, and for a while, things got better. More peasants and craftsmen came and were able to produce some goods. However, it took a lot of work to prosper as the Company pushed them to repay the costs of transporting them there. By the winter of 1609 and 1610, things went wrong again.

The relationship with the Powhatan natives was ruined, and the exchange of food stopped. They ran out of supplies and ate all of their stock. Soon, they had nothing to eat, and it was a very cold winter. By the time it was over, only 60 people had survived.

However, the Virginia Company was determined to make their endeavor prosper, so they brought new people and a new governor who could lead the settlers in a much better way. They had learned that tobacco, a crop widespread in America, could make a lot of money. It was a new product in Europe, and its demand was growing. So, they decided that Jamestown would become a tobacco producer.

In 1619, the company brought women to the village to help make the colony flourish. Therefore, the lonely settlers would soon have families, and the town would become a real community. Shortly after, they brought more hands to work the crops. In 1620, the first ship with enslaved African people arrived in America to work in the tobacco fields.

Within 40 years, Jamestown stopped being a weak village on the brink of collapse and became a thriving colony. Soon, Jamestown expanded the lands under their control, and the territory was named Virginia.

THE COLONISTS: WHO WERE THEY?

The Pilgrims

Virginia, originally called Jamestown, was founded to become a trading point. The settlers and the company took a long time to accomplish that goal, but eventually, the colony survived. Nonetheless, there were other reasons why people left England and moved to America.

In 1620, a group of about 100 people embarked on a ship called the Mayflower and started a 65-day journey to America. They were searching for a new life but also looking for a place where they could practice their religion freely without fearing for their lives.

After the English Protestant Reformation, the only official religion in Great Britain was the Church of England, which the King was the leader of; this group of people did not agree with this. They were Protestants but differed from the Church of England, so they decided to resettle. They gained the permission of the British monarch to establish a colony in the new lands in North America.

Crossing the ocean in the 1600s was a dangerous adventure. The journey was full of threats like raging storms and ruthless pirates. Even so, this group of people embarked and headed to Virginia.

They got lost when they approached the coast, and the ship sailed north. They landed in Plymouth, where there was no sign of British settlers. There, they would start their own colony.

It was a small group of people, but many of them were families, unlike the group that came to Virginia. Soon, the population started to grow. A baby was born on the Mayflower while they were going to America. The baby was a boy, and he was named Oceanus. After they landed, another woman gave birth to another boy. He was named Peregrine.

When they arrived, the new settlers signed a document called the Mayflower Compact. This was the foundation of the colony and its own government. It was an early expression of their will to govern themselves that had great influence in the colony of Massachusetts that developed later.

As soon as the Pilgrims arrived, they started building their town. The first years were very hard, and only a few survived. However, in the autumn of 1621, they were able to have their first harvest, which was greatly celebrated. This was later considered the First Thanksgiving.

Although their goal wasn't to run a business, economic endeavors were very important to them. They had to build up the communities and ensure survival, which wasn't an easy task. However, their Protestant beliefs encouraged them to work hard for their neighbors and to progress. Therefore, settlers were dedicated workers, and after great efforts to hold the colonies, they started to grow. Soon, they produced and exchanged goods with England and other European countries.

After the Pilgrims, many other people ran away from religious persecution in Europe. Those who followed the Protestant religion were forced to leave countries where the official religion was Catholic. In the following years, more Protestants from England and Europe came to America.

The Farmers

After the first wave of immigration, more people moved to the American colonies. While in the beginning, most of them were people who could afford the trip and searched for new opportunities to make money, many others came with nothing. Farmers and peasants were very important in the colonies. Not only because they would produce the goods to exchange with the Natives and with Europe but also because they produced the food the settlers needed to survive.

Delaware was one of the Middle England colonies that developed agriculture. The colonization process began with the Dutch and Swedish settlers. Later, the British took control of the lands, enabling agriculture to prosper. People cultivated wheat, barley, Indian corn, and peas. They also had living stock and farm animals: pigs, sheep, goats, and cattle.

The Dickinsons were one of those people. The family was the third generation of landowners and had a tobacco plantation in Maryland. In 1740, the family moved to Delaware to work on new lands and replaced tobacco with grains. The son, John Dickinson, continued his education in his new home. The comfortable economic situation of the family allowed John to have good training in many fields.

He learned about crops, trading, and laws. As an adult, John Dickinson took control of the family's plantations, administered the properties, and was in charge of the enslaved laborers who worked for him. He went to Philadelphia to study law and become an attorney. After a while in London, he came back to practice.

Soon, he was involved in politics. He was the speaker of Delaware's provincial legislature to represent the voice of the farmers who had made the colonization process possible. John used the local newspapers to write down his ideas about how the colonies should be governed and to express the farmers' demands.

The Businessmen

When the British first came to America, they were looking for business opportunities. The first immigrants were predominantly businessmen or nobles who wanted to use their money to run a business in the new lands. Therefore, many of the first settlers were businessmen. Nonetheless, not all of them were successful.

In 1722, Samuel Adams was born in Boston, one of the most important cities in flourishing Massachusetts. The colony wasn't founded for business purposes, but it became an important economic center of the British possessions in America.

Massachusetts was placed along a big bay that was filled with harbors. The abundance of timber and fish allowed the settlers to live not only on farming. The intense activity in the harbor and the frequent trade with Europe led to an early development of the industry. The settlers manufactured supplies for the harbors and ships.

Samuel belonged to a religious family, like many others in Boston. His father was a deacon in the local church, but Samuel was more interested in business. After studying at Harvard, he tried to open a business of his own, but things didn't work out. So, he was employed as a tax collector, but that wouldn't be a good option either because his job clashed with his values.

He had learned within his family the moral values of their faith: personal and civil virtue, which implied getting involved in the matters that affected his community. People in Massachusetts, predominantly Protestant, had a great sense of self-governance and were active participants in the colony's politics. Therefore, Samuel himself became a politician.

After a frustrated career as a businessman, Samuel decided to focus on politics. He became a member of the Massachusetts House of Representatives and the Boston Town Meeting. Samuel was concerned about the situation of most people in Massachusetts involved in trading.

Even though trading was growing, there were good harvests, and the industry helped progress, most people were workers with middle-range incomes. Mainly, the English were becoming rich. That's why Samuel couldn't fulfill his duty of collecting taxes, as they were harmful to the neighbors of his own community.

The Lawyers

People who arrived in America were pursuing different dreams. Many of them had fled from their countries in Europe because they wanted freedom to practice their religion. That had been the case with the Pilgrims who came on the Mayflower and founded Plymouth, Massachusetts. People from other religions, mainly Protestants, settled in the different colonies.

Among the refugees, a family of French Calvinists settled in New York. The youngest son was called John, and his surname was Jay. You will need to remember him because he's one of the fathers of our nation. He was born in 1745. By then, the city was thriving and changing.

New York soon became one of the most populated cities with a busy and thriving economy. The Dutch, the first settlers, had developed intense fur trading between the local populations and other colonies. The farmer families learned to grow crops in the valley of the Hudson River and had large plantations. Then, after the British seized the colony, they brought enslaved people to also work in the plantations and produce more.

The settlers traded those goods produced in the plantations and sold them to the European countries. Therefore, trading became a very important activity. That boosted the appearance of liberal professions and jobs that helped trading and business.

To be good at trading, you need to be able to understand the law. People had to sell, purchase, own lands, and administer their properties. Therefore, lawyers were very important. At first, businessman used their common sense to understand the English laws that framed their activities so they could know what they could and couldn't do. However, as the city grew, law schools were opened. In New York, the King's College (in the present day, University of Columbia).

When John was a young boy, his mother taught him at home, but after his 14th birthday, his parents decided to send him to college. At first, John didn't want to attend college. However, he soon realized he didn't want to be a farmer. He liked the rhythm of the city near the harbor. He wanted to help people to look after their rights.

As trading grew, lawyers gained prestige in all the colonies.

Lawyers became more and more important as businesses increased. Businessmen needed lawyer's services to ensure they wouldn't be cheated or break the law. There were many clients for the new lawyers. Therefore, a lot of young men born in farmer immigrant families decided to study law. One of them was John Adams. His great-grandfather emigrated from Essex, England, to Massachusetts in 1638, one of the first waves of settlers. Therefore, John Adams's family were pioneer settlers in Massachusetts.

John's father was a church priest and a soldier, and they also had a farm with crops and stock. However, in the 1760s, men found other interests and job opportunities. Then, John studied at Harvard, where he learned about laws, business, and philosophy.

His father expected him to become a minister like himself. John didn't want to be a minister. Instead, he started teaching after graduation and soon found out he could have a professional career as a lawyer. He had earned a reputation among his colleagues and had plenty of clients. His father wasn't pleased about his son's choice, but it was all set.

Nonetheless, John wasn't completely satisfied with his decision. He was the first man in the family who didn't join the army. He didn't know yet that he would eventually become a military hero.

TIES ACROSS THE ATLANTIC: THE BRITISH POWER

As we have seen, the British crown promoted the first colonies, and the first ships with settlers that arrived in America belonged to trading companies. However, soon after they settled, the colonies expanded their territory and organized thanks to the settlers' hard work. That allowed them to develop an active economy and grow. This favored the colonies but also the kingdom.

The role of the British was important in the early stages as they brought supplies to support the settlers. The British also defended the colonies from the Dutch and Spanish attacks and dominated the local populations to expand the lands. The negative part of this was that the colonies weren't free.

A colony is a land portion conquered and ruled by another distant country. The people who live there are called colonists and must obey the ruler of that other country. This means the colonists could own, work, and produce in their lands. However, they had to obey the king of Great Britain and accept the British rules.

Even though many colonists were born in America, the population of the colony wasn't a free nation. They had a handful of rights, such as running their own business and buying or selling properties. However, there are many differences between them and those who lived in Great Britain. For instance, Americans didn't have the opportunity to participate in the government, collect their own taxes, and decide how to spend that tax money.

Great Britain was an empire ruled by a king. Therefore, it was the only one with power and legitimate rule over all the Empire's territory, including the colonies. However, as of 1689, Parliament in England was the institution in charge of making the rules, not the king. In Parliament, the people of the kingdom could choose their representatives to speak for them and express their concerns. People in the colonies didn't have that chance.

Each colony had a charter that explained the link between them and the King. That document said that the people of the colonies recognized themselves as subjects of the King of Great Britain, and in exchange, the King provided protection and assistance.

On the other hand, since the colonies had been the idea of the British monarch and the main purpose was trading, the Empire had the right to benefit from American goods and work. The colonist could own their lands, enslaved laborers, the goods they produced, and earn money from their economic activities. However, the king still had the right to request a percentage of it. This percentage was collected through taxes.

Even though the colonists weren't allowed to participate in the British government, they had their own institutions to debate and make decisions on the local issues in the colonies. Each colony had an assembly where the citizens could participate. Nonetheless, the governors were directly elected by the King, and there were some subjects that the colonists couldn't decide on. Taxes was one of them.

Key Points

- The British established their first stable colony in North America in 1607, and it was Jamestown.
- After many troubles, Jamestown survived and expanded and became the first British colony in America: Virginia.
- Between 1622 and 1732, the British established 13 colonies on the East coast of North America, on the shore of the Atlantic Ocean.
- The first expeditions were carried out by trading companies promoted by the British King.
- The Pilgrims and other colonists were refugees running away from religious persecution.
- Farmers and businessmen worked and built up the colonies. They grew crops, took fish from the rivers and the sea, timber from the woods, and exported them to Europe or exchanged them with Native populations.
- John Dickinson was a farmer and landowner from Delaware.

- Samuel Adams was a businessman and politician from Boston, Massachusetts.
- John Jay and John Adams were lawyers. Jay was from New York, and Adams was from Massachusetts.
- A colony is a territory conquered and administered by another state.
- Colonists don't have the same rights as the state's citizens.
- The British colonies in America had a charter with the British King or Queen accepting their authority.
- The colonies had assemblies to discuss life in the colonies, but they couldn't decide anything on a large scale.
- The British Parliament established the rules and laws for the colonies, and the crown could charge their trade with taxes.

CHAPTER 2
THE FRENCH AND INDIAN WARS—THE AFTERMATH

The relationship between the settlers and the British king was good enough. The two parties benefited from that relationship. The Empire had goods to trade from the colonies, and the settlers were free to run businesses and have some independence to choose their local authorities.

The settlers and the Empire lived in peace for about a century and a half. That situation eventually changed, and the settlers decided they wanted control over their own destiny. The spark that lighted the conflict was between two European empires arguing for lands in North America. A war between Great Britain and France would have unexpected consequences for everybody...

THE SOLDIERS

By the middle of the 1700s, the 13 colonies were already settled, and they were all thriving, but the good run wouldn't last.

Along with farmers, businessmen, and lawyers, soldiers were the other important social group within the colonies. The army's job in the colonies was first to defend the settlers from the attack of the other nations that wanted to conquer the same lands. Later, when the expansion began, they also forced the native populations to move away from the new lands.

Being a member of the army was a great honor. You might remember that John Adams felt he had disappointed his family by not being a soldier. Every man in his family had been in the army. However, life in the colonies could make businessmen become farmers and make anybody become a soldier at any moment.

There was a man who always knew that he wanted a military career. He was born in 1732 to a wealthy family that owned a farm in Virginia. He inherited the property and ten workers to make it prosper. He became a farmer himself to expand his lands. Nonetheless, he was determined to be a military commander; his name was George Washington.

When George was 20, his brother Lawrence died. He served in the Virginia Militia. George thought it was the opportunity to enter the military. Therefore, he became a soldier. Soon after, he had his first mission. At that moment, he had no idea it was the first spark that would light up the American Revolution.

THE FRENCH

Before the British successfully settled in North America, the French had established some colonies in present-day Canada and the south of North America. Despite the occupation of the coastal lands by the British, the French wanted more lands on the continent. Therefore, the French king ordered his troops to install a camp on the west side of the British in the valley of the Ohio River. The colony of Virginia claimed those lands.

Lieutenant Colonel George Washington received the order to go to the frontier of the British colony and persuade the French to go away and leave British lands (although formally, those lands were under Native people's control). Washington made a great impression on his superiors as he quickly reached the frontier and started negotiations with the French forces.

By then, the French had already built up forts in the territory. Washington ordered his troops to do the same, and soon, there were forts of both empires on each side of the border. Neither of them wanted to leave their positions.

When the British arrived, Washington met the French commander and gave him the Virginia governor's message to leave the lands. The French denied the claim and insisted on staying there. Washington returned with the answer to his authorities, knowing the matter hadn't ended there.

THE NATIVE PEOPLE: THE IROQUOIS NATION

Several tribes inhabited the Ohio Valley, many of them British allies. Most of them were unified in what was called the Iroquois Confederation and under the power of the Iroquois. The British had even given the title of "Half-King" to his leader Tanaghrisson.

These Native populations were very concerned about the presence of the French in their lands but were also suspicious of the intentions of the British that continued to surround and occupy their lands. The Iroquois were British allies but also had their own interests there.

One day, George Washington was walking with Tanaghrisson from one fort to another when they found a French camp beyond their border. The French commander, Jumonville, tried to explain to Washington that it was a peaceful mission using a translator because they didn't speak the same language.

Tanaghrisson didn't speak any of them and misunderstood the presence of the French there. So, he assumed that the camp was a surprise attack and killed Jumonville. That unleashed a global armed conflict between the French, the British, and the Native people in the colonies and between the French and British empires in Europe.

THE FRENCH AND INDIAN WAR OR THE SEVEN YEARS' WAR

Washington understood that the incident would bring a strong response from the French. Since Tanaghrisson was with him, the French would assume that they were allies and that the act of war came from the British. Therefore, Washington hurried to strengthen the walls of his fort and prepare to defend the lands. However, the French moved quickly with a Native American army as allies. They attacked Washington's defenses and defeated them.

Washington retreated and sheltered in Fort Necessity, in lands claimed by the colony of Pennsylvania. There, the French and their Native allies reached Washington and confronted him in the Battle of Great Meadows.

When the French and Indian War started, John Adams felt guilty for not being a soldier. He attempted to go to war and prove his courage, but instead, he remained working as a lawyer. His moment hadn't arrived yet.

Despite the initial defeat, Washington continued to fight as a volunteer. He got his revenge in the Battle of Monongahela. On that occasion, Washington wasn't in charge of the operation, but the English troops were under heavy fire from the French. All the commanders were killed or severely wounded. Then, Washington assumed the leadership of the frightened soldiers and guided them to evacuate the battlefield and survive. That gained Washington the name of "hero of Monongahela" and the rank of colonel with 1200 men in charge in the Virginia militia.

GROWING UNREST: TAXES, LAWS, AND LIBERTY

The French and Indian Wars took place in Europe and in the colonial possessions of both countries in Asia and America. It started in 1754 and ended in 1763 with the Treaty of Paris. Even though the outcome favored Great Britain, it brought many long-term consequences.

The Treaty of Paris resulted in many negative decisions for the colonies, and as we saw, the colonists weren't invited to the negotiation. The British monarch, King George III, and Parliament set the rules, and the colonies could do nothing about it.

One of the conditions to put the war to an end was that the British colonies could not attempt to expand their territory in the west into Native Americans' territories. Besides, the British court blamed the government of the colonies for the conflict as it had started due to a failed maneuver from the Virginia Militia (under Washington's orders). The king thought the colonies couldn't defend themselves, which meant they would need more help and troops from the imperial army.

On the other hand, Great Britain was the ultimate winner of the war and had gained a lot of territory in the west of the colonies, but there was a lot to regret. The war had cost a fortune. Half of the expenses had been used to fight the French in North America.

King George III was satisfied to have kept his colonies and defeated his historical continental enemy, the king of France, Louis XV. Nonetheless, he had to find a way to recoup all the money he had spent. His first idea was to raise taxes for British citizens, but it soon brought social unrest within his own land in England. Therefore, he decided that if the colonies had caused such expenses, it would be fair that they paid for them.

Therefore, the British Parliament decided to put new taxes on the American colonists.

As you might imagine, the colonists didn't welcome these decisions. As they were not allowed to expand their territories, this meant that their growth was very limited. This decision impacted merchants and businessmen who chose not to invest more money in the colonies as they had done in the past. The landowners thought they couldn't have more plantations and produce more. The fur trade that was so important in New York moved to Montreal (Canada) and took away a lot of important trading activity from the colony.

The British had come to defend the colonies from the French and perhaps saved them from an armed conflict with the Native populations, but it wasn't such a good thing. The Empire could protect the colonists, but it meant many negative consequences that the king would ask to be paid back. The colonists couldn't make their own decisions and were pointed out for failing in their defense, and then they were punished with taxes.

The colonists faced many dangers and threats, lived isolated from the known civilization, and suffered from hunger and illness to serve the king's interests. After all those sacrifices and a war they had fought, they were paid back with higher taxes. How unfair!

The lawyers wouldn't just sit back and take what was going on. John Jay and John Adams prepared to react and defend the colonists' rights. Businessmen and landowners were determined to protect their interests; after all, they supported trading that benefited the crown as much as themselves. Dickinson and Adams were ready to use their place in the local assemblies to raise their voices on behalf of the colonists. George Washington had learned important lessons from his first experience as a military leader.

Everything was ready for the colonists to start walking their path to liberty.

Key Points

- Soldiers played a vital role during the colonization process. George Washington left his plantations to serve in the Virginia Militia.
- Washington was given the mission to stop the French from building a fort near the colonial borders. They were trying to occupy lands claimed by Great Britain.
- Native American people who lived in the Ohio River valley were allies of the British, while others joined their enemies.
- A confusing incident started a war between the French, the Native American populations, and the British. It was called the Seven Years War or the French and Indian War.

- Things went very wrong for Washington and his troops.
- In the end, the British won and signed the Treaty of Paris in 1763.
- The Treaty established that the colonies couldn't expand their territories into Native American people's lands.
- The war was very costly to the British Empire, and King George III decided to raise the taxes in Great Britain and put new taxes on the American colonists.
- Social unrest raised in the 13 colonies.

CHAPTER 3
THE ROAD TO REVOLUTION

THE SUGAR ACT: THE BEGINNING OF TROUBLE

One of the pillars of colonial trade was the possibility to buy and sell with any other nation in the world. To run a successful business, people had to be able to sell their goods to anyone who would want to buy them. Similarly, they needed to be free to purchase goods from other colonies and countries at the best price.

After the Seven Years' War, the British king needed to increase the income of his kingdom. Therefore, he attempted to control the colonies' trade with other nations.

The British Empire had colonies in other parts of the world, like southern Asia and the Caribbean. The king wanted to force the colonies to import goods only from other British colonies instead of other countries like The Netherlands or France. To accomplish that, he enacted a new rule to control the origin and destination of the products that entered and left the colonies.

One day in 1764, John Jay was at his studio in New York and received a new client. The man owned a refinery where sugar was turned into rum. This was an alcoholic beverage very cherished in Europe and by the British all over the world. The refineries were some of the most thriving industries in the colonies, especially in New York.

This man explained to John that when he took his barrels to the harbor, a member of the customs office had made him declare how much rum he was delivering, who bought it, and how much he had paid for the raw material. The man refused to provide all that information but was surprised to learn that the taxes he paid for the sugar were lower.

Another man entered the office and interrupted the conversation. He was a fisherman, and when he tried to sell his products to a French company, he learned at customs that the state kept part of his profit. That tax was new!

Jay had heard about the new tax policy the king attempted to implement but wasn't sure what it meant. So, he went to the customs office to ask. He was told that the Sugar Act had been established for the colonies there. Lower taxes for the importation of sugar coming from other British colonies would boost the refinery industry, and everybody would benefit from the measure. That way, rum producers didn't have to buy smuggled sugar to avoid paying the high taxes.

It didn't look that bad. However, the act had many other consequences for the colonists. The taxes that were taken off from the sugar were put on many other goods just as important as rum for the colonies' trade. The colonists had to pay higher taxes when they bought products from other countries, but they also couldn't sell their goods to whomever they wanted. As soon as he read the Sugar Act sent by the British Parliament, Jay knew he would have a lot of work in the following months.

When John Dickinson ran into a neighbor in Delaware, he was on his way to the local government's office. The man was a timber producer who had just heard about the new legislation. Until then, he had sold his timber production to French, Dutch, and English companies. Since he needed to get the most money from the sale, he wanted to sell it to the one willing to pay more. According to the Sugar Act, he could only sell it to a British company, and they could sell it abroad.

Dickinson thought it was directly against the natural rights of any human being, even those living in a colony. A man should have full rights to their property and decide what to do with it for their own benefit. Dickinson decided to act.

He thought people needed to know what was happening and decided to publish a pamphlet. He believed the Sugar Act and all the taxes it put on the colonists were against the individuals' rights. He also asked the British Parliament to listen to the colonists' needs. Dickinson said taxes imposed on the colonists who couldn't participate in the debate were unfair and against Great Britain's law. If the colonists had to pay more taxes, they should have a seat in Parliament and be able to take part in discussions.

Dickinson became famous among the 13 colonies for his ideas, and a lot of people agreed with him. Some years later, John also wrote *Letters from a farm in Pennsylvania to the Inhabitants of the British Colonies* and essays published in a newspaper in Pennsylvania. That's how people shared their ideas with the community, and it was very important in the revolutionary process. John Dickinson's ideas inspired many people to fight for their freedom.

John Dickinson wasn't the only one who raised his voice against the king's decision. Samuel Adams was by then a member of the Town Meeting in Boston. He led the opposition to the Suger Act that was held in Boston and in the colony legislature in Massachusetts.

Samuel Adams claimed that the charter the colonies had with the king allowed them to set rules and taxes for the colonies themselves. If the colonists were denied those rights, it would be the same as considering them as slaves. He also argued that the colonies should stay together to confront the king's power and questioned the authority of the British Parliament over the 13 colonies.

With their pamphlets and speeches, Dickinson and Adams planted the seed of the revolution.

THE STAMP ACT

On June 24th, 1765, John Adams was reading the Boston Evening Post when he found a complaint from the people of New York against the new acts. A year ago, the British crown had imposed the Sugar Act, and it seemed there was a new one: The Stamp Act.

John used to write essays on politics for several Boston newspapers, and as a lawyer, he thought he needed to learn more about what the act meant. Soon, clients would begin to visit John for advice and legal representation. To learn more about The Stamp Act, he went to the House of Boston. There, he was informed that there was a new tax for everyone in the 13 colonies.

The new tax was a Treasury stamp. This stamp was a seal that was put on any legal document, for example, an appointment to the office, a newspaper or pamphlet to publish, and many other documents that people used in their daily lives.

This new tax had a great impact on every financial activity in the colonies. For instance, buying and selling lands demanded filling and signing a lot of documents, and after the Stamp Act, people had to pay for each of them. Things called commercial papers and promissory notes were common, especially during sales. Now, all of them had to pay the new tax. If a person needed to collect a debt, they needed a particular document... which they'd now have to pay a stamp tax for. Every aspect of life would be more expensive due to the new tax.

The Sugar Act directly affected those who bought or sold goods abroad. The Stamp Act was another tax within the colonies and affected everybody. By using taxes, King George III attempted to make the inhabitants of the colonies pay for the expenses of the war the Empire had fought to defend them.

People's reactions against the measure were rapid. Everybody in the colonies was aware of the relationship with the king and the Parliament's authority to control their activities, including trading. Nonetheless, adding taxes on the colonies' population was beyond that authority.

Lawyers, politicians, and writers published their ideas in the press and in pamphlets to reject the act. Orators and common people expressed their opposition in public places. Everybody was determined to demonstrate that they would not accept the act. They said the act treated the colonists as slaves, accused the king of acting like a tyrant, and shared this motto: "No taxation with no representation."

The population was angry because the king attempted to force them to pay taxes, but they didn't get anything in exchange. The colonists wanted to be treated as the rest of the kingdom's citizens, with the same civil and political rights. If they had to pay taxes, they deserved to be a part of the government and decide their own rules. Until now, the idea of stopping being a colony wasn't a part of the plan. However, once social unrest grew, the path to revolution unfolded and wouldn't stop.

People first reacted by holding public demonstrations in front of British offices and riots in all 13 colonies. However, the events in Boston escalated even further. Sometimes, the demonstrations became violent. The colonists were very angry. Traders, craftsmen, lawyers, and politicians all gathered in the streets to express their opposition to the Stamp Act.

Adams, Dickinson, and others believed that violence wouldn't solve the problem. Instead, violent demonstrations and riots would only lead to more severe problems. Time would prove they were right. However, they didn't discourage people from letting the British government know they wouldn't accept any law or tax the king wanted to impose on them.

THE TOWNSHEND ACTS

Despite the increasing unrest in the 13 colonies, King George III was determined to collect money from the colonies. The crown needed resources to pay the debt left by the war. Far from listening to the colonists' demands and complaints, the British government continued to enforce new tax regulations.

The first one was the Sugar Act in 1763, and then the Stamp Act in 1764. Despite the strong opposition to the measures in the colonies, the British Parliament established new taxes on other products: lead, glass, paper, paint, and tea. From then on, the colonists would have to pay more when those products arrived in the harbors.

This series of new tax regulations was called the Townshend Acts. Parliament and King George III were trying to show sturdiness and power in front of the colonies and the subjects. Nonetheless, the colonists wouldn't back down from their resistance.

This time, the population's reaction in the colonies was even stronger. Each time, more people took part in the demonstrations, and things went out of control. Massachusetts was the colony where the conflict became the most complicated.

A group of people from Boston organized to defend the colonists' rights by any means. They were called the Sons of Liberty. They were a secret group, and they plotted against the current government. They used to gather under an old elm tree near the Boston Common.

In 1765, the Sons of Liberty led a protest against the Stamp Act. They made a dummy of the stamp collector who was in charge of implementing the new tax in Boston. They took the figure and hung it from a branch of the elm tree. The figure had a sign with a message that said, "What greater joy did ever New England see than a stamp man hanging on a tree!"

A crowd joined the demonstration. They took the figure and went to the public officer's house, where they wreaked havoc. The tree symbolized the colonists' struggle and was called the Boston Liberty Tree.

Samuel Adams and John Dickinson were ready to defend the colonists' rights, but they were very concerned about the violent events that had taken place. In opposition to the Stamp Act, the mob had destroyed the houses of British public officers. Therefore, Adams, as a representative in the Massachusetts legislature, proposed a different strategy to force the king and Parliament to review and reconsider the taxes.

In his letter, Adams called the population of the colonies to make a boycott of British goods. They wouldn't buy anything that reached the ports coming from other British colonies or traded by a British company.

The boycott strategy reached all the colonies, and women played a key role. Women were in charge of the household budgets and decided the daily purchases. Moreover, many of them ran businesses and started producing the things they used to buy from the British. That way, the boycott would be possible, and the population wouldn't lack the essential components for survival.

THE BOSTON MASSACRE: A CITY ON EDGE

Massachusetts was the first colony to publish a complaint against the new taxes. Then, New York and South Carolina followed. Later, all of the 13 colonies opposed the king's policy. The British merchants soon started to feel the boycott's impact as their sales dropped drastically.

This one wasn't the only protest action. The Parliament and the colonial governors (elected by the king) decided to close the colonial legislatures. There, men like Dickinson and Adams were spreading their ideas and calling together the population to oppose. The colonists didn't accept this decision and continued their reunions in other places. The British authorities had great trouble controlling the colonial population.

On the other hand, violence hadn't ended. When the Stamp Act was launched, the people of Massachusetts burst into the officers' houses and caused havoc. The officers felt intimidated and resigned before distributing the stamps. After the Townshend Acts and while the rest of the population carried out the boycott of British goods, a group of people continued to provoke the customs officers by vandalizing their houses. Some people did more than just carry out the boycott; some continued with violent practices, riots, and public demonstrations and were called "radicals."

The situation became critical for the British merchants and commissionaries in all the colonies, especially in Massachusetts. Therefore, the local British authorities told the king to send more troops to the colonies and restore order.

In October 1768, the royal army landed in Boston. The army's presence in the colonies had always been looked at with suspicion by the colonists. They considered that the use of violence was against the individuals' rights. Within the current context, the army's presence looked like a new effort of the king to control the colonists: first, with taxes, then by using force.

The presence of the army added more tension to the city, where the radicals, many of them members of the political group Sons of Liberty, started to act against their neighbors. The radicals chased those who wouldn't join the boycott or continued to buy goods from British merchants. The radicals put a sign on stores and houses that said "importer."

One day, a customs officer named Richardson tried to take out the sign from his neighbor's shop when a group of young radicals attacked him. Richardson and another man armed themselves with muskets and fired against the attackers. One of the shots hit an 11-year-old boy named Christopher Seider. A crowd took part in the young boy's funeral, increasing the tension in the streets guarded by the British soldiers.

Samuel Adams published many letters and essays in the local newspapers questioning the presence of the British troops. He was one of the organizers of the boy's funeral and claimed to be a victim of British tyranny. The boy's death increased the tension between the local people and the soldiers.

On March 5th, a voice spread the news that the British soldiers would cut down the Liberty Tree. A crowd of hundreds of angry colonists walked towards the Town House of Boston. On King Street, a group of nine soldiers ran into the mob and fired. As a result, five people died, and another six were wounded. This event is remembered as the Boston Massacre.

Samuel Adams led the people to gather in an assembly and ask the authorities to send away the troops. The governor decided to take the soldiers involved in the revolt on trial. John Adams was one of their attorneys. Although Adams defended the soldiers accused of murder, he argued that they shouldn't have been there in the first place. The jury only found two of them guilty, but the trial was used as proof that Massachusetts could govern itself.

For a while, things calmed down in Boston.

THE BOSTON TEA PARTY: A BREWING REBELLION

For a while, the conflicts in the colonies softened. Between 1771 and 1772, news from across the Atlantic Ocean fueled the colonists' anger again. The salary of the governor and the judges of the Superior Court wouldn't be paid by the colonies anymore but directly by the crown. The money for those salaries would be obtained from the taxes on tea.

Tea was one of the most important goods produced by Great Britain, and it was sold all over the world. While the other taxes imposed by the Townshend Acts were eliminated, the tax on tea was kept. The colonial merchants avoided the tax by buying smuggled tea from Dutch companies.

Once more, the British crown needed to gain more control of colonial trading and collect more money from taxes. In 1773, the British Prime Minister authorized a shipment of thousands of pounds of tea from the East India Company. The Company had a lot of tea that needed to be sold immediately to avoid bankruptcy. Therefore, the crown gave it a monopoly on the American colonies' trade.

The ships would reach the ports of Boston, Charleston, New York City, and Philadelphia. The East India Company wouldn't have to pay taxes at all. Instead, the merchants of the colonies would have to pay a high fee. The protests arose again, and the merchants refused to accept the tea shipment.

Not too long ago, Boston had been the center of the resistance to the Stamp and the Townshend Acts. Now, in Boston, the governor ordered three East India Company ships to dock and the locals to pay the taxes. This decision lit up the spark of revolution again.

The Sons of Liberty prepared for a new protest. On December 16th, 1773, a group of about 50 men from Boston, members of the Sons of Liberty, disguised themselves as Native American people by covering their faces with soot and charcoal. They approached the harbor at night, where the three British ships, the Beaver, Dartmouth, and Eleanor, were waiting to unload the shipment.

The Sons of Liberty boarded the ships and dropped 342 tea boxes into the sea. Within a few hours, the whole shipment of tea from the East India Company had sunk. The Company had lost almost 10 thousand pounds, more or less 2 million dollars today.

The news of the episode in Boston's harbor spread through the other colonies. The rebellious actions carried out by the Sons of Liberty inspired others to act. In New York, the locals refused to let the British unload the tea. In Pennsylvania, people gathered to stop the ships from approaching the dock.

The Boston Harbor incident would later be named the "Boston Tea Party" and is considered the moment when the American Revolution began. The colonists had taken extreme steps to fight the tyranny of the British.

A few months later, news of what happened to the East India Company ships in Boston, New York, and Philadelphia reached Great Britain. Instead of changing the tax regulation, the king and Parliament responded with more oppressive actions.

The new laws were called the Coercive Acts. The crown decided to close the harbor of Boston and change the Charter between Massachusetts and the crown, disbanding the colonial assembly forever. Massachusetts had to pay the East India Company for the money lost with the destroyed shipment of tea.

The king sent more troops to seize Boston. The new governor moved the seat from Boston to Salem and had extended powers that allowed him to restrict people's rights. For instance, Bostonians didn't have the right to gather anymore.

Samuel Adams, the revolutionary leader, took action. He sent letters to the assemblies of the other colonies and soon received positive answers. Soon, the first continental Congress was scheduled for September 1774 in Philadelphia, Pennsylvania.

Key Points

- According to the Carters (the agreements between the colonies and the king), the colonies could create rules and taxes for themselves.
- The colonies didn't have representation in the British Parliament.
- In 1763, the British Parliament imposed a new tax on the colonies. It was called the Sugar Act.
- The act lowered the taxes on sugar but added new taxes on other products, such as fish and timber, that the colonial merchants traded.
- In 1764, Parliament put a new tax on the colonies. It was called the Stamp Act, which implied that any document required in the colonies had to pay a Treasury stamp. Every economic activity became more expensive in the colonies, and the measure affected everybody.
- John Dickinson and John Adams rejected these taxes and published their ideas in the press.
- People were very angry at King George III and the Parliament. The colonists didn't ignore their authority but demanded "No taxation without representation." If the colonies had to pay more taxes, the colonists deserved to be represented in the government.
- Demonstrations and riots against the Acts started in the colonies, mainly in Boston.
- Dickinson called for people to boycott and stop buying British goods.
- The answer from the crown was more and higher taxes. Moreover, King George III sent troops to Boston, where the opposition to the Acts was stronger.

- On March 5th, 1770, a crowd went to demonstrate in front of the Town House of Boston. There, nine royal army soldiers confronted the crowd and opened fire. As a result, five people were dead and six wounded. It is remembered as the Boston Massacre. It was the expression of British brutality and the king's tyranny.
- In 1772, the British Parliament authorized the East India Company to sell a huge shipment of tea in the 13 colonies. The Company wouldn't have to pay anything, but the merchant colonists would have to pay the tax when they received the load in their harbors.
- On December 16th, 1773, a group of 50 members of the Sons of Liberty organization boarded three ships of the East India Company in the Boston harbor. They dropped all the tea load into the sea, causing enormous losses. Later, the incident was called The Boston Tea Party.
- The protest was copied in other colonies, such as New York and Pennsylvania, where people didn't allow the ships to unload the shipment.
- In response to the Boston Tea Party, the crown closed the harbor in Boston and moved the seat of the government to Salem. The new governor restricted the civil rights of the colonists. More troops were sent to Boston.
- Motivated by Samuel Adams, the colonies decided to gather at the first colonial Congress in Philadelphia.

CHAPTER 4
THE BATTLES BEGIN

The events in Boston alerted the other colonies. Could the king send his troops to the other cities? The colonists needed to be prepared. They had to find a way to force the king to negotiate and remove the taxes.

Therefore, the colonists gathered to discuss and decide what to do.

However, the British also paid attention to what was happening in the colonies. While the locals were searching for a way to resist British power, the king and Parliament would try to keep the colonies under control. So, things were about to get even more difficult.

THE FIRST CONTINENTAL CONGRESS

The news from Boston reached Virginia. There, George Washington wrote a paper to protest against the Coercive Acts sent by the British authorities. He believed it was unjust to close the harbor of Boston and occupy the city with military forces.

However, the people of Virginia's local government considered it was not enough. Was it possible that the British could do the same in Virginia?

There was a man who was particularly concerned for the colonists' rights in Virginia. His name was Patrick Henry. He was a member of the Virginia House of Burgesses and was very upset about the British's use of taxes and other measures. Henry gave a speech against the Stamp Act when it was established, and after the Coercive Acts, he was determined to do something.

Henry contacted John and Samuel Adams in Massachusetts and decided to gather people from all the other colonies and make a collective decision. They would gather secretly to avoid any action from the British. Then, Virginia sent an invitation to the colonial governments of the other colonies.

Each colony elected delegates that would represent them. The meeting would take place on September 5th in Philadelphia, Pennsylvania. Although the invitation reached all the colonies, Georgia didn't approve of taking part. When the day came, the 52 delegates from the 12 colonies gathered in Carpenter's Hall in Philadelphia, and the First Colonial Congress started. It was later known as the First Continental Congress. The meetings took place between September 5th and October 26th, 1774.

The colonies were very different. Some were bigger and were more populated. Therefore, not all of them had the same number of delegates. However, they decided to give one vote to each colony to ensure equal representation when they reached a decision. Unity and solidarity among the colonies was the most important thing.

The First Continental Congress was an assembly. The delegates presented their ideas and arguments, and then they would vote to make a decision that they would all support. The president of the assembly was Peyton Randolph. He was from Virginia and was Thomas Jefferson's cousin. George Washington was a good friend of his.

Among the delegates, Patrick Henry, John Adams, and Samuel Adams already had the idea of using this event to gain independence from British power. John Dickinson, George Washington, and John Jay were also part of the Congress. Although they were all concerned about the acts passed by the British Parliament, not all were sure about breaking the bond with the British completely. However, they all agreed that they wouldn't stand the British oppression without resistance.

The meeting was secret because the colonists discussed the issue of imperial power. The British authorities couldn't know about the Congress. The delegates from the colonies had to decide how they would react if the British closed other harbors, imposed new taxes, or sent more military forces.

Meanwhile, Benjamin Franklin, a famous scientist and inventor from Boston, was in London. He had traveled to protest against the Stamp Act. When the Congress met, he remained in Great Britain to take a message to King George and the Parliament on behalf of the people of the colonies.

The debates among the delegates took seven weeks. The main issue was how the colonies would respond to the British violence in Boston and the Intolerable Acts. Some delegates argued that a violent response would escalate the problem rather than find a solution. Therefore, they suggested a different tactic.

The colonists discussed a new boycott of British goods to force the imperial government to accept and respect the colonists' rights. On October 20th, the Congress established the following:

- They would create an association among the colonies and act together.
- The colonies wouldn't buy or accept British goods in the colonial ports if Parliament didn't take the Coercive Acts back.
- The colonies were open to communicating with the British authorities to achieve an agreement.
- The Congress would meet again in Philadelphia on May 10th, 1775.
- The colonies needed to prepare an army in case the British government didn't agree to negotiate. The First Continental Congress chose George Washington, an experienced military leader, to be the chief commander of the colonial army. He traveled to Massachusetts to organize the troops.

Even though the colonists gathered in the Congress still believed peace could be achieved, the conflict was far from over. Many things would happen before the delegates met again for the Second Continental Congress.

LEXINGTON AND CONCORD: THE SHOT HEARD ROUND THE WORLD

The Boston Tea Party had made the British very angry. Parliament had imposed the Coercive Acts on Massachusetts, and, in addition, the authorities were after the men accused of leading the assault on the British tea shipment. In April 1775, British troops in Massachusetts were looking for Samuel Adams and John Hancock. They were to be arrested for ordering the attack on Boston Harbor.

John Hancock was a businessman from Massachusetts who had been a delegate in the First Continental Congress. After the Stamp Act, he had been one of the promoters of boycotting British goods. He even bought and sold smuggled goods as a way to protest against the tax. Samuel Adams suggested him to be a member of the local government.

Later, Hancock was accused of smuggling by the British. John Adams was his lawyer and avoided prison. However, Hancock and Adams were pointed out for their anti-British actions.

In December 1774, John Hancock was elected again to represent Massachusetts in the Second Continental Congress. However, a lot of things happened before this.

John lived in Boston when the Tea Party took place. Since it wasn't a safe place anymore, he decided to move to Lexington with his father. On April 18th, 1775, he received the news that British troops were heading to town to look for him and Samuel Adams. They were accused of planning the Boston Tea Party.

In Boston, the same group that carried out the Boston Tea Party was still organized and prepared in case the British would strike back. One of them, Paul Revere, had organized a secret network to spy on The Redcoats (the British soldiers). He wanted to detect any unexpected movement of the royal army.

One day, he heard of the operation set to arrest Adams and Hancock and took a heroic decision. On April 18th, Paul Revere left Boston and went to Lexington, a nearby town, to alert the Patriots that The Redcoats were preparing to come after them.

Revere borrowed a horse and left at night towards Lexington. He rode in the middle of the night, narrowly avoiding getting caught by the British. At midnight, he reached Lexington, where Adams and Hancock were hiding. Revere told them that The Redcoats were marching to seize them and that he had already warned the Patriots.

By the time The Redcoats reached Lexington, the Minutemen were waiting for them. About 70 militiamen who had joined the revolutionary cause were prepared to open fire.

None of them were professional soldiers. Most of them were farmers from Acton, a town in Massachusetts. They had organized a militia to defend the community from the British if anything like the events in Boston took place. They had learned to use the musket and the bayonet and developed the ability to prepare quickly. That earned the name of "minutemen." That morning, they honored that name.

They were led by a man called John Parker. He was a farmer from Lexington who had fought in the French and Indian War and now had joined the revolutionary troops. Although he was severely ill, he marched to lead the Minutemen that morning of April 18th. He had told his men, "Stand your ground. Don't fire unless fired upon, but if they mean to have a war, let it begin here."

The Redcoats and the Minutemen confronted each other outside Lexington around 5 in the morning. It was a moment of great tension. Nobody moved. The British and the Patriots had their weapons charged. Suddenly, a British officer shouted, "Disperse, ya rebels." At first, some of the Minutemen began to retreat after their commander, John Parker, ordered them to disperse. But then, a shot was fired.

Even though nobody knew who took that first shot, both sides opened fire. The result was eight American soldiers dead and another ten wounded. The rest of the Minutemen stepped back. The Redcoats had won, but the Patriots would take revenge. As Parker had said, if there was going to be a war, it should start there.

The victorious British army continued their ride to Concord. General Gage knew that the Patriots had weapons and ammunition there, and they would take them. Once more, the local people were warned by Revere and others who had spread the news. They had warned the villagers that about 800 Redcoats approached the town searching for weapons and ammunition.

The British finally arrived in Concord and searched where the revolutionaries had hidden their military supplies. They couldn't find anything. The villagers, promptly warned by Revere, had taken the stuff to a safe place. Without accomplishing the mission, The Redcoats prepared to leave town.

Outside Concord, Acton Minutemen commanded by Captain Isaac Davis awaited. They could see The Redcoats marching in columns back to Boston. Davis prepared to attack. As the troops approached the line crossing into Concord, Davis turned to his men and gave them the option to leave. Nobody was forced to risk their lives on a battlefield. They weren't soldiers. They were just men trying to protect their community and defend themselves from British oppression.

Despite Davis's offering, none of the Militiamen left. They were all determined to fight.

The Minutemen avoided encountering The Redcoats while they were marching through the road. Instead, they separated and moved through the forest by the road without being seen by the British. The Minutemen had a plan.

Davis and his people settled at the Concord Bridge. There, they would wait for The Redcoats. When the British approached the bridge, they could see The Minutemen marching down the hill. Perhaps it wasn't a professional army, but they marched as if they were. Many soldiers were walking together and holding their weapons, ready to fire. The British were intimidated because they didn't expect such an encounter.

The British general ordered his troops to retreat and occupy the other side of the bridge. The Redcoats prepared to defend themselves. When both armies were in front of each other, a British officer from Concord ordered, "For God's sake, fire!"

Right after, the Minutemen answered the fire and killed three British soldiers. Nine others fell wounded. That was called "the shot heard around the world." This shot and the combat it started is considered the beginning of the American Revolutionary War.

The British retreated and continued their march back to Boston. That battle at North Bridge in Concord was the first time the British troops were forced to retreat. They had lost several soldiers and didn't find the revolutionaries' supplies. The mission was a complete failure, and it still wasn't over.

All their way to Boston, the British were chased by the Minutemen. John Parker and his men were waiting for them when they passed Lexington. They sought revenge for those who had been killed by the British that morning when they had decided to retreat.

Parker's troops were hidden in the forest, at the sides of the road. When the British passed, the Minutemen militia fired at them and caused several casualties. The rest of the British Army escaped and made it to Boston. John Parker wouldn't live long after that battle. He died in September of that same year. Still, he had made his contribution to his nation's freedom.

The unplanned battles in Lexington and Concord began a new stage of the conflict. While the First Continental Congress was gathered in Philadelphia, the delegates still believed there was a possibility the king would listen to their demands. Instead, in Lexington and Concord, the colonists' militia had proven they weren't afraid to confront the royal army. However, The British have shown they would do anything to stop them and impose order on the rebels.

THE SECOND CONTINENTAL CONGRESS

As soon as Revere brought the news of The Redcoats going to Lexington and Concord, Hancock, and Adams wanted to join the militia and fight. Nonetheless, they were eventually persuaded to escape.

In May 1775, the Second Continental Congress gathered again as the First Congress scheduled it. The delegates from the colonies gathered at the same place in Philadelphia. This time, the 13 colonies sent their representatives, even Georgia.

The news of the events in Lexington and Concord had reached Georgia. Although a big part of the population wanted to remain loyal to the king, many other colonists realized they needed to join the other colonies for protection. Therefore, they decided to join the Congress.

After running away from Lexington, Samuel Adams and John Hancock joined the rest of the delegates. Hancock was elected president of the assembly this time. Some delegates were also members of the First Congress, and others were new. Benjamin Franklin and Thomas Jefferson were among the most remarkable names who joined in 1775. They would play a vital role in the rest of the revolution.

Benjamin Franklin had just returned from London to attend the meeting in Philadelphia. By then, Franklin was a well-known inventor and scientist and had been on diplomatic missions in England and France, searching for support for the colonists' rights.

Franklin was born in Boston, but he moved to Philadelphia. In the Congress, he represented Pennsylvania. He would soon go back to London to speak on behalf of the colonists. Franklin tried to reach an agreement with the British Crown as long as the King and Parliament agreed to respect the colonists' demands.

In addition to George Washington, who had already been a part of the First Continental Congress, the delegation of Virginia included Thomas Jefferson, the man in charge of writing important documents.

Jefferson was a young political activist and Virginia House of Burgesses member. From the beginning, Jefferson suggested a radical position. He felt that there was no point in trying to reach an agreement. He had always expressed public opposition to the taxes the British imposed on the colonies. After the Intolerable Acts of 1774, Jefferson encouraged a boycott of British goods in Virginia, and in Congress, he proposed independence.

At first, the delegates didn't want to speak about independence yet. They believed there were other options to solve the crisis. However, the battles in Lexington and Concord persuaded many that freedom was the only possible way. The British didn't seem willing to negotiate.

The Congress had a lot to discuss and decide. Meanwhile, the congressmen were in charge of the political decisions for the 13 colonies. However, the British still had power, so there were two parallel governments in the colonies.

The Congress decided they would organize and train their own army. It was the Continental Army, which had already been formed in Massachusetts under the orders of George Washington. From then on, the massive recruitment of soldiers began in the 13 colonies.

Congress had the power to make decisions about borrowing money, negotiating with other nations, establishing a postal service, and all government functions.

Meanwhile, in each colony, opinions were divided. Some people supported the revolutionaries. Many others defended the British power over the colonies. The political group Sons of Liberty, who had carried out the Boston Tea Party attack, spread to other colonies beyond Massachusetts. They encouraged all those who wanted to fight for freedom to join the Continental Army and organized local colonist governments.

THE BATTLE OF BUNKER HILL: A PYRRHIC VICTORY FOR THE BRITISH

After the battles in Lexington and Concord, the British returned to Boston and settled their camp there. On the patriots' end, men from the neighboring colonies of New England came to Massachusetts to join the Minutemen and the revolutionary militia. They came from Rhode Island, Connecticut, New Hampshire, and what today is the state of Vermont.

The British had suffered several casualties in their failed mission to imprison the rebel leaders in Boston and seize their supplies. General Gage was concerned about stopping the colony's revolutionary forces. More troops arrived in Massachusetts in June, and Gage had a new plan to defeat the colonists.

Meanwhile, George Washington, the Continental Army's chief commander, headed to Boston with his troops. He also had a plan to strike the British. He would try to take the city under British control from the heights of Breed's Hill at the Charlestown peninsula. At the top of the hill, the Continental soldiers built a fort, and from there, they confronted the British. That place was later called Bunker Hill.

Washington's men began working during the night. They raised a wall atop the hill with pickaxes and shovels. From there, the soldiers could cover the British settlement of Charlestown and the Harbor. About 1,000 men from Massachusetts gathered at the fort to confront the British.

General Gage and the other British generals were astonished to see what the American soldiers built in such a short time. Gage thought it was very dangerous to have the revolutionaries so close to Boston and decided to attack and make them leave the peninsula.

On the evening of June 17th, the troops led by General Gage marched in strict order towards the hill. They started climbing the slopes of the hill without breaking their lines. The Continental soldiers waited at the top behind the fort. Aware of their limited supplies, Officer William Prescott ordered them not to fire until the British were close enough. They didn't want to waste bullets. But when the British got close, they fired!

The British didn't stop after the first wave of bullets. They continued to climb the mountain while under a hail of gunfire, even over the bodies of the wounded men, time after time. After the third wave of gunfire, the American soldiers had run out of ammunition. The British finally succeeded in reaching the wall and broke the Americans' defense.

The battle continued with hand-to-hand combat using bayonets and swords. It is a bloody battle. There were hundreds of casualties on both sides. British reinforcements arrived, and the Americans were vastly outnumbered. There was no hope for the Continental soldiers in that fort anymore; those who could, ran away.

When the battle was over, groups from both sides that didn't take part in the fighting awaited in nearby hills. Both sides prepared for a counterattack. Nonetheless, both armies were exhausted, and nobody attacked again that night. The British army returned to their garrison in Boston, and the revolutionary army returned to their camp outside the city.

The British had won the battle at Bunker Hill at a great cost. Over 1,000 British soldiers died or were wounded that night in the Charlestown peninsula. On the Continental Army's side, 400 casualties were counted. Besides the outcome, one thing was clear: The Americans proved that this wasn't a momentary rebellion. It was a revolution.

THE SIEGE OF BOSTON: A LONG STANDOFF

After the events in Lexington and Concord, George Washington moved to Boston. He grouped the militia, settled a camp, and built a trench surrounding Boston. It was his new strategy: a siege. The Continental Army would isolate the British troops in Boston and force the Empire to negotiate.

The British had strength in the city, with over 4,000 men. The Royal Navy controlled the harbor. Yet, they were enclosed by the Patriots.

Meanwhile, the Continental forces grew. After the battles of Lexington and Concord, people from all the colonies offered themselves to serve under Washington's orders. The army began with about 6,000 men.

Within the following months, it reached 16,000 soldiers. The main target was to keep the British enclosed in Boston. Eventually, they would run out of resources, and the siege wouldn't allow the British to resupply them. However, the British could still receive help by the sea as they controlled the port.

On the other side, the British prepared to defend themselves. General Gage received the reinforcement of generals John Burgoyne, Henry Clinton, and William Howe and their troops. They gathered their forces in Boston, leaving the Charlestown peninsula unprotected. Nonetheless, the British didn't believe the Patriots could attack there again. Besides, the British had navy support if such an attack happened.

Even though each side had succeeded in keeping their position, the generals of both armies faced great challenges. In Boston, the British generals had to deal with the food shortage. It took very long for supplies to arrive. In the countryside where Washington's army camped, they had to survive a harsh winter.

There was another problem. The Continental Army enlisted soldiers for one year. There wasn't enough money to pay them a stable salary. What would happen if the war took longer? How would Washington retain his men and stop them from leaving the army?

By the end of winter, Washington had an opportunity to make a move and end the siege with a victory for the Americans. Washington was looking for a chance to launch a massive attack on the city, but it wasn't easy. In late January of 1776, Colonel Knox arrived at the camp. He came from Fort Ticonderoga. He brought with him cannons and artillery that the Continental Army desperately needed.

Now, Washington had an excellent chance to put pressure on the British. He ordered the cannons to be placed on a peninsula in front of the harbor. Then, they built a new fort very quickly. The British only knew about it when it was complete. That made the British think the Patriot army was larger than it was.

At that point, the British generals were worried about their situation. They didn't want to repeat the battle of Bunker Hill that caused them so many casualties. Without reinforcements and facing a bigger army than they had expected, they weren't very hopeful. Therefore, they sent a note to Washington with a proposal.

The British offered to leave Boston without destroying it first if the Americans left them to sail away without being attacked. Washington eventually accepted the offer, as it meant regaining Boston, putting it under the Patriots' control.

The siege of Boston started in April 1775, after the battles in Lexington and Concord, and ended in March 1776. The British eventually moved the army from Boston to New York.

Key Points

- After the Boston Massacre and worried about the British reaction to the Boston Tea Party attack, the colonies organized the First Continental Congress. The colonists wanted to take action to force the British to remove the Coercive Acts, known as the Intolerable Acts.
- The Congress gathered in Philadelphia, Pennsylvania, between September 5th and October 26th, 1774. The colony of Virginia was one of the promoters, and all the colonies except for Georgia sent their delegates.
- The Congress decided that they would attempt to force the British to negotiate by boycotting their goods. In addition, they ordered the organization of their own army, making George Washington the chief commander.
- They also decided that the next Congress would take place in May 1775.
- In April 1775, the British forces started a military operation to seize the Patriots' weapons and ammunition from a farm in Concord. The British also pursued Samuel Adams and John Hancock, who were accused of planning the Boston Tea Party.
- Paul Revere used his spy network to discover the British plan and rode to warn Adams and Hancock. On his way, he told everybody in the towns to prepare to fight as the British were coming.

- On April 18th, the British approached Lexington, and a group of 70 militiamen called Minutemen waited for them. The British commander ordered them to disperse, and while the men did so, a shot was fired.
- Nobody knew who fired first, but a skirmish began, leaving eight American soldiers dead and another ten wounded.
- The British continued their way to Concord, where they couldn't find the hidden weapons. Instead, they met with a troop of Patriots at North Bridge in Concord.
- The British officer ordered them to open fire, and a new battle started that day.
- Later, the British started withdrawing, but the Patriots followed them on their way back to Boston.
- The Minutemen of Lexington waited for them hidden in the forest and attacked as the British passed.
- Once the British arrived in Boston, the Patriots settled outside the city. Shortly after, Washington reached there with the Continental Army, and the siege of Boston began.
- The Patriots took the Charleston peninsula and built a fort in Bunker Hill. The British attacked them on June 17th. The British eventually won that battle but with over 1,000 casualties.
- The Americans held the siege. Meanwhile, the Second Continental Congress took place in Philadelphia.
- The siege of Boston reached a turning point when Colonel Knox arrived with cannons and artillery. Washington's army was ready for an attack, so the British asked for a truce and evacuated Boston.

CHAPTER 5
THE STRUGGLE FOR INDEPENDENCE

While George Washington was fighting in Massachusetts to force the royal troops to surrender, the Second Continental Congress was gathered in Philadelphia. Patriots from all the colonies joined and settled local governments to reinforce the boycott of British goods. However, the situation was complicated.

It wasn't easy for the colonists to survive without British goods.

The representatives of the colonies had different opinions in Congress. Many of them preferred to reconcile with Great Britain. They wanted to return to their initial plan: involvement in Parliament to discuss and decide their own rules and taxes. Only the radicals supported the more extreme decision: ending the colonial bond with Great Britain and becoming an independent nation.

THE DECLARATION OF INDEPENDENCE: A NATION IS BORN

The Last Attempt to Reconcile with the King

was in the summer of 1775, and the congressmen were reunited, discussing the following steps. Some believed the problem was the British Parliament and not the King. After all, the taxes had been imposed by the Parliament. Therefore, they suggested reaching out once more to King George and trying to find a peaceful solution.

Thomas Jefferson, a man with a lot of political experience, offered himself to write the letter. It would be a formal petition to tell the King that the colonists wanted peace and to return to having a good relationship. After working on the document, Jefferson read the draft to the rest of the assembly.

Mr. Jefferson, the Virginia man, had always advocated for independence and freedom, so his letter was rather hostile. The other members of the assembly thought the King wouldn't welcome it. Then, the draft was reviewed and edited by John Dickinson, a representative from Pennsylvania. He changed the document's tone and attempted to show the King that the colonists wanted peace and the restoration of a good relationship.

Mr. Dickinson, and John Jay the lawyer from New York, represented the conservative side within Congress. Their main goal was to achieve representation in Parliament without separating from the British Empire. At least, this was when the conflict began. As things turned more violent, they searched for peace before anything else.

Thomas Jefferson and John Adams, a lawyer from Mass-achusetts, were the leaders of the radical wing. Instead, they believed that the only solution was to end the colonial bond.

However, the conservatives won the vote on that occasion and sent the King a petition calling for peace. After Dickinson's changes, the document said that the colonies remained loyal to the British King and were willing to negotiate. The colonists offered the King some options to consider. This document is known as the *Olive Branch Petition*.

On July 8th, 1775, the members of Congress signed the *Olive Branch Petition*, which was finally sent to the King. None-theless, the same Congress signed another document, the Declaration of the Causes and Necessity of Taking Up Arms, the following day. The Congress had taken the role of govern-ment over all the colonies, and this document explained why the colonists were forced to go to war.

This second document opposed the *Olive Branch Petition*. It was a difficult situation for the Patriots to handle. On the one hand, they wanted peace and to stand up for their rights. On the other hand, the British attacked them and forced them to fight. The battles of Lexington and Concord made many conservatives change their minds and become supporters of independence.

Months passed, and the Congress didn't receive a response to the Olive Branch Petition. The congressmen continued discussing how to move forward. One morning, a royal declara-tion arrived, and John Hancock, the president of the Second Continental Congress, read it to the rest of the assembly. It was called the Declaration of Rebellion.

In that declaration, King George III declared the colonists rebels and ordered every British officer, military and civilian, to defend the Empire and do everything they could to end the rebellion. All the leaders of the rebellion, that is, all the men gathered in the Congress, were charged with treason and would be sentenced to death by hanging.

Everybody was shocked. Most wanted peace, but now, it seemed they couldn't step back. They had been accused of treason, and the British justice system would prosecute and punish them.

Jefferson and the other radicals realized that this declaration had reduced the colonists' options. If there had been two sides before, now, there was nothing left but the Declaration of Independence. However, they knew that the 13 colonies needed to agree on that. That was the only way to become a free nation and confront the power of the Empire.

In December 1775, things became more complicated for the colonies. The British Parliament passed the American Prohibitory Act, which banned trading between Great Britain and the American colonies, and colonial ships would be treated like enemies. The Declaration of Rebellion and the Prohibitory Act were considered by many a declaration of war by the Empire on the colonies. As a response, the colonies opened the ports in April 1776.

The Road to Freedom

Thomas Paine was a writer and publisher born in England but moved to America. By 1775, he had settled in Pennsylvania and became the editor of the Pennsylvania Magazine. Through this magazine, he published essays sharing his political ideas. He always was a champion of liberty.

By the end of 1775, Paine was concerned about the events in Boston and the battles between the Patriot troops and the royal army. He wanted to join the cause of liberty and find a way to help. So, he decided to publish a manuscript. Paine believed in the colonies' independence and wanted to let people know what that meant and explain to them why it was the only option.

In January 1776, Thomas Paine published a pamphlet called *Common Sense*. In it, he explained what independence meant in easy language, which was enlightening for people who had only ever known being ruled by a foreign king.

Paine talked to citizens who were surprised and frightened by everything that was going on. In the last years, after the French and Indian War, they had been forced to pay higher taxes, more royal troops had come to the colonies, and now, the King's army was attacking them, as it had in Lexington, Concord, and Bunker Hill.

The pamphlet discussed individuals' rights and why an inherited monarchy was the worst government. It said that every society has the power to create a government to provide security. It urged the colonists to have their own government based on a new system called democracy.

Common Sense by Thomas Paine made everybody think and talk about independence. That's why it is considered one of the most influential documents that gathered widespread support for the patriots.

However, even if more citizens became supporters of independence, the decision still had to come from the Continental Congress gathered in Philadelphia. There, the delegates from the 13 colonies had to reach an agreement.

The Declaration of Independence needed the approval of the 13 colonies. The new nation should be born into a democracy, which should be done by debate and agreement.

The assembly assigned Thomas Jefferson the task of writing the Declaration of Independence. After he finished, John Adams and Benjamin Franklin were asked to review it. Every word had to be carefully selected as the declaration would decide the destiny of a new nation. Finally, after some time, the document was finished.

After days of discussions, the president of the Congress held the vote on July 2nd, 1776. President Hancock read the declaration and asked each of the representatives from the 13 colonies if they agreed to it. The result of the vote was that 12 of the representatives agreed, and one representative did not agree. The New York delegation claimed they were still waiting for further instructions and, therefore, wouldn't define their vote. That meant their vote wasn't either for or against; Instead, they declined the opportunity to vote.

Nonetheless, the result of the vote was overwhelming. 12 of the 13 colonies had said yes to becoming a free nation and breaking free from the British Empire's control.

The Declaration of Independence stated:

- That delegates were gathered on behalf of the citizens of the colonies.
- The United Colonies declared their right to be free.
- The control that the British Crown had on the colonies was to come to an end, or something along those lines.

- As free states, the United Colonies had the power to declare war and peace, trade, and have their own rules.

The final Declaration of Independence was read and signed by 56 delegates representing the 13 colonies on July 4th, 1776.

KEY FIGURES OF THE REVOLUTION: MEET THE FOUNDING FATHERS

Thousands of people took part in the journey that gained the 13 colonies freedom and independence. Some were involved more directly, expressing their ideas and opinions in the press and raising their voices in government offices. Others joined the patriot troops early on and fought the first battles to accomplish freedom. Citizens played an important role in the boycotts and demonstrations.

Gaining independence would not have been possible without these people. It was a big win for all of the citizens of the 13 colonies. It was a collective triumph of the people of the 13 colonies. Nonetheless, some of the men involved in this process are considered the Founding Fathers of our nation because they made important contributions to the creation of the United States as a free country and a republic.

George Washington

George Washington was the military leader of the patriot army. As the commander of the Continental Army, he led the troops in battle, ensuring victory.

In Boston, he was able to organize the patriot army even though the men weren't professional soldiers and didn't have military training. Washington's troops eventually succeeded despite the many shortages they faced. The British Army had to surrender and leave Boston, ending the siege.

Later, Washington led the Continental Army in the most important military campaigns. Whenever he fought, he ensured victory, and each of them was one more step to independence. He faced many challenges, such as a lack of food and military equipment. Even though he faced these challenges, he could still keep the spirit of the army alive, even when it was difficult.

Thomas Jefferson

When most people doubted, Thomas Jefferson spoke of freedom and democracy. From the beginning, he stood up for independence and did everything he could to convince others that it was the best option.

He was a politician and a diplomat who not only worked for independence in the colonies but also searched for support in other nations of the world.

Jefferson wrote the Declaration of Independence when he was only 33 years old. Later, he became the leader of the Republican party when political parties appeared in the United States.

He was against a central government and continued to defend the right of the states (the colonies in the past) to choose their own government.

John Adams

This lawyer became an important figure in the revolution during the events in Boston. He defended the British soldiers who fired against the crowd in what was called the Boston Massacre.

Even though he defended the British, he used the trial to expose his ideas of self-government. He argued that those soldiers should have never been there. The trial was later used to prove that the colonies were, in fact, able to carry out justice by themselves.

Later, Adams was elected as the delegate from Massachusetts. In Congress, he became one of the leaders of the radical wing. He helped review the final draft of the Declaration of Independence.

Benjamin Franklin

He advocated for the colonists' rights long before the revolutionary process began. Benjamin Franklin first published his ideas under a nickname in Boston and later in Pennsylvania.

In 1775, he was elected to represent the colony in the Continental Congress. John Adams chose him to be in the Committee of Five, which was created to write the Declaration of Independence. Even though Jefferson eventually wrote it, Franklin helped to review the draft.

He made a significant change in the first lines. Where it said, "We hold these truths to be sacred and undeniable," he wrote, "We hold these truths to be self-evident." It meant that there was nothing more important than laws.

Alexander Hamilton

Born in England, Alexander Hamilton moved to America and settled in New York in 1772. Shortly after arriving, he felt he could identify with the American cause and became an advocate of the New Yorkers' rights.

In 1775, he joined the local militia as a volunteer and became an artillery company captain. He was a soldier of the American Revolution and also helped review the draft of the Declaration of Independence.

Hamilton played a key role in the organization of the new nation and was one of the writers of the Federalist Papers.

John Jay

He was one of the members of the First Continental Congress representing the colony of New York. He wrote and published a paper called Address to the People of Great Britain. Although he advocated for the colonists' rights, he promoted the end of violence and a peaceful ending to the conflict with the Empire.

He was also a member of the Second Continental Congress, although he wasn't there when they signed the Declaration of Independence. Instead, he went back to New York to organize the local government. Later, he cooperated in writing the Federalist papers and helped organize the new government of the United States as a free country.

Even though John Jay is less famous than other fathers of the nation, his silent participation was very important for the United States.

James Madison

James Madison actively participated in the political life of Virginia. He was a member of the Virginia Assembly and helped write its constitution there. He was also a delegate to the Continental Congress.

Madison was one of the writers of the Federalist Papers, along with Hamilton and Jay. With his contributions, he helped to approve the constitution of the United States as a free country.

Although he was an active member of the debates before the Declaration of Independence, his greatest contribution was in the following stage, when the colonies became a free state.

THE CONTINENTAL ARMY: SOLDIERS OF FREEDOM

After the Declaration of Independence, a statue of King George III was torn down as a symbol of freedom. The Patriots made good use of the statue. The metal was melted and used to make 42,000 musket bullets. The independence had been approved in a congress but had to be defended on the battlefields.

Before war broke out between the colonies and the British army, each colony had a militia, except for Pennsylvania. These militias weren't professionally trained to enter a war.

Militiamen were part of the colonial defense against possible attacks from the French and the Native American people. However, they were just part-time soldiers. They weren't professionals. When the Revolutionary War began, the Continental Congress hurried to organize its own troops.

Massachusetts was the first colony to organize its militia properly. This was because of the events that happened in Boston. They created companies(military units) of minutemen, as they were expected to respond at a minute's notice. The Minutemen played a crucial role in the Lexington and Concord battles. The other colonies started gathering their militias as well.

Later, Congress formed the Continental Army in 1775. George Washington was assigned as the chief commander of the new army. At that moment, it wasn't a professional army. Some soldiers belonged to the militia, but most were civilians with different backgrounds who joined to fight for independence. The first mission of the Continental Army was to surround the British army in Boston, putting the city under siege.

Although soldiers came from the 13 colonies, most were from New England. The average age was 20, but there were men between 15 and 40. They were farmers, merchants, craftsmen, and Native American and African American men. About 231,000 men served in the Continental Army. Among them, about 6,600 were enslaved people who fought for the colonies' independence and their personal freedom.

At first, they all used different uniforms, but later, they were changed to blue to distinguish themselves from the British soldiers who wore red. The revolutionary troops had muskets that could be loaded 3 or 4 times per minute. That is fast, but the American muskets were considerably less effective than the rifles of the British soldiers. To fire, American soldiers had to be 100 yards away from the enemy to have a chance of hitting them; the British soldiers could fire at 300 yards, which gave them a significant advantage. However, muskets allowed soldiers to have bayonets, a blade used in hand-to-hand combat.

At the beginning of the conflict, at the end of 1775, the Continental Congress authorized men to enlist for a year. After the Declaration of Independence, the Patriots understood that the conflict would extend, and soldiers were allowed to enlist for three years.

George Washington gave the Continental Army the shape of a professional army. It wasn't only essential to achieve victory in front of the British; Washington believed that the army was important to developing a new American identity. Being a soldier and fighting for independence would turn those men into free citizens of the new nation.

WOMEN OF THE REVOLUTION: UNSUNG HEROES

The path to freedom wasn't only built by the male colonists. Women played an essential role in all the stages. For example, women carried on the boycott strategy to force the British Parliament to set back the taxes.

However, many women had a special role in the American Revolution:

Abigail Adams

Abigail Adams was John Adams's wife. She wrote letters to him, sharing her feelings and giving him advice. Abigail believed in independence but was also concerned for women's rights. She was one of the first people to share her views against slavery.

While her husband was on a diplomatic mission in Europe, she was left to look after their farm, the family's money, and the education of their son, John Quincy Adams, the future president of the United States.

Mercy Otis Warren

Mercy Otis Warren was a writer and playwright who dared to publish her political ideas in the press. At first, she wasn't against the British government, but after the Sugar and Stamp Acts and the events in Boston, she changed her mind. She became very involved with the Patriots' cause.

She wrote pamphlets and essays in the Massachusetts Spy and the Boston Gazette. She wrote plays about British tyranny and how they mistreated the colonists. Later, she was one of the first women and historians to publish documents on the American Revolution.

Betsy Ross

Betsy Ross was a young widow who owned an upholstery business in Pennsylvania. She also worked for the Continental Army, preparing soldiers' uniforms and other supplies.

In the summer of 1776, George Washington and other officers of the Continental Army visited her at her shop. Washington carried thirteen red and white stripes and thirteen stars. He asked Betsy to sew them and make a flag for the colonies fighting to become free.

Betsy Ross is credited for making the first American flag.

Mary Ludwig Hays

Mary Ludwig Hays was better known as Molly Pitcher. Like many other women, she went with her husband, who joined the Continental Army. Women accompanied the men of their families and stayed near the military camp. They took care of different issues to help the soldiers. Molly and the other women washed clothes, cooked for the troops, and provided medical help.

Molly fought in the Battle of Monmouth in 1778. First, she carried water to the soldiers, but then she replaced her husband on the battlefield. Molly's husband was wounded, so she grabbed his musket and went to the battlefront.

Margaret Corbin

Like Molly, Margaret joined the Continental Army following her husband. She took a place on the battlefield and was severely wounded during combat. Eventually, she survived. She was the first woman in the history of the United States to receive a pension as a war veteran.

Phillis Wheatley

Phillis Wheatley was an enslaved African American woman who lived in Boston in the 1770s. She wrote poetry. Phillis was the first woman in America to have her writings published.

Her poems were about freedom and people's spirit, and she dedicated a poem to George Washington. Phillis had the opportunity to read the poem to Washington himself while the Continental Army was holding the siege on Boston.

Sibyl Ludington

Sibyl Ludington became heroin during the American Revolution when she was only 16 years old. In 1777, she lived in New York and found out that the British were planning an attack on the Continental Army in Danbury, Connecticut.

As soon as she learned about the plan, she rode her horse for 40 miles and avoided capture. She reached Putnam County, New York, and alerted the Continental Army. Even though the British succeeded in Danbury, the Patriots were able to force the British to retreat.

Key Points

- The Second Continental Congress was gathered in Philadelphia. At the same time, the battles of Lexington and Concord were fought, and the Patriot army held the Boston Siege.
- The Congress made a last attempt to reconcile with the British Crown. Thomas Jefferson and John Dickinson wrote the Olive Branch Petition, asking King George III for a peaceful solution to the conflict.
- In August 1775, the King passed the Declaration of Rebellion, ordering every officer to rise against the

rebel colonists. The rebels would be judged and sentenced to death.

- In December 1775, the British Crown stopped trading between Great Britain and the colonies.
- Thomas Paine wrote 'Common Sense', a document encouraging people to fight for freedom.
- The Congress discussed and decided to declare independence. Thomas Jefferson was assigned to write the declaration.
- The assembly voted for the Declaration of Independence, and 12 of the 13 colonies approved it. Only New York's delegation abstained (decided not to vote).
- Among the many people who fought for independence, some men are considered our nation's Founding Fathers for their unique contributions to independence. They are George Washington, Thomas Jefferson, John Adams, Benjamin Franklin, Alexander Hamilton, John Jay, and James Madison.
- The Founding Fathers were members of the Continental Congress, fought the Revolutionary War, expressed and taught the political ideas that led the colonist population to fight for freedom, and built the republic after the Declaration of Independence.
- The Continental Army, led by George Washington, was formed by militiamen and citizens who joined to fight for freedom. The Continental Army ensured victory and became an important element of the identity of the new nation of the United States.
- Women played important roles during the American Revolution. They participated as writers, artists, and soldiers. Some women who played a special role

during the revolution were Abigail Adams, Mercy Otis Warren, Mary Ludwig Hays, Margaret Corbin, Philips Wheatley, and Sybil Ludington.

CHAPTER 6
TURNING THE TIDES

The Declaration of Independence Act was adopted by every colony. People's anger had increased since the events in Lexington and Concord and the siege of Boston. People from all the colonies joined the Continental Army.

Meanwhile, the British set fire to the towns of Falmouth, Massachusetts, and Norfolk, Virginia, to get back at the rebel colonists for their anti-British actions. This did nothing but upset the colonists more and fueled the cause of the revolutionaries. It also gained sympathy for the Americans among the British enemies. The Spanish and the French sent supplies to support the rebel colonies.

After the Declaration of Independence, the people of the colonies split their opinions. Some of them wanted to maintain their relationship with the British Crown. They were called loyalists because they remained loyal to the King. They thought that remaining a part of the British Empire was more convenient. They had the royal army's protection and also received economic benefits. From their point of view, the Continental Congress's actions were illegal.

Nonetheless, many others supported the revolutionaries. In some colonies, both sides fought against each other.

Colonel Washington had moved the Continental Army to New York after the victory in Boston. The British troops had escaped from Boston, but Washington believed they would soon come back and probably land in New York. Therefore, he had to prepare to face and beat them. And he was right.

THE BRITISH ATTACK

King George sent 130 warships and a 25,000-soldier army to New York and set up camp on Staten Island. Washington moved the troops to Brooklyn Heights on the other side of the river and prepared to defend. Days passed, and Washington, with the Continental Army, was ready for combat, but the British didn't attack.

One day, the British eventually opened fire on the Americans' position. There were a lot of casualties on both sides, but the British Army had split up, and a second branch had surrounded the Continental Army.

George Washington was determined to defend their position, but being attacked on two sides, there was no option but to retreat. But the Continental Army became trapped between the British infantry and the river before they could retreat.

While the British Army was fighting the way it was trained as a professional army, for many of the American men, it was their first time on a battlefield. Most of them didn't know what to do. They were courageous but had little military training. Even though Washington had worked to prepare them, the heat of the battle caused a lot of confusion among his troops.

The British caused 300 casualties on the American side and captured 1,000 men. The revolutionary soldiers had difficulties in keeping their lines to defend properly. The situation in the Continental Army was very delicate, and when the rebel soldiers realized they had lost, they eventually panicked and ran into the forest to save their lives.

The Continental Army, or what was left of it, retreated to Brooklyn Heights. Washington needed a plan. They were surrounded by the British and trapped.

Fortunately, luck was on Washington's side, and nature gave him an opportunity to save the army. While the British started digging to build a siege around the Continental Army, a deep fog covered Brooklyn Heights. During the night, Washington led his army to escape through the river from Brooklyn to Manhattan.

After the fog disappeared, the British realized what had happened and chased them as they fled. Finally, Washington could take the army to a secure place in New Jersey. There, he'd have enough time to regroup the troops.

Soon, winter came. The British settled their camp in New Jersey. They had brought troops of mercenary Germans as reinforcements to fight against the rebels. Mercenary soldiers didn't fight to defend their nation. Instead, they fought for money. The Continental Army had also settled in New Jersey, on the west coast of the Delaware River.

Nobody expected an attack during the winter, which gave Washington an idea. The troops' spirit was low, and the colonel thought they needed a reason to believe in the revolution. He decided to make a risky decision.

In December 1776, Washington realized that the Continental Army's situation was critical. Then, Washington made a bold decision: He would attack the enemy in the middle of the winter when nobody was alert. He decided to cross the icy waters of the Delaware River with 2,400 soldiers. They would launch a surprise attack on the German troops supporting the British.

It was an almost impossible task. The river waters were nearly frozen, and the steam made sailing towards the opposite shore difficult. The soldiers and the horses they took with them were cold and frightened. The wind was blowing, and it began to snow while they were going through the river. It was terrible conditions for combat.

It took them all night to reach the shore. The rebel soldiers led by Washington were poorly equipped to fight in the middle of the winter but still moved on. They were heading to the town of Trenton (New Jersey) to attack the unaware British allies. On the morning of December 26th, 1776, Washington led the Continental Army's main body against the German merce-naries camped at Trenton. After a brief battle, Washington's men captured almost all the enemy without losing many Amer-ican soldiers. The battle significantly boosted the Continental Army's weakening morale and inspired more people to join the cause. The Continental Army was victorious again.

This successful maneuver, led by Washington, sent a message to the American Patriots: the war wasn't over yet, and there was hope.

THE BATTLE OF SARATOGA: A CRUCIAL VICTORY

In 1777, the British were determined to recover the colonies. The British had succeeded in taking Philadelphia, and the Congress had escaped to York. However, the North Continental Army would fight a battle that changed the course of the war.

While British General Howe struggles to take and hold Philadelphia, the northern British army moves from Canada to try to take the Hudson Valley. The British commander, General Burgoyne, had the order to invade New England to separate these colonies from the rest.

Nonetheless, the Patriots were aware of the possible attack. George Washington had assigned General Horatio Gates to lead the Northern section of the Continental Army. Gates and 9,000 soldiers had settled on the highlands of Bemis Heights, near the village of Saratoga and the Hudson River. General Gates was supported by General Benedict Arnold.

Gates had ordered his men to build a fort on the hills. It was a wall about 4,000 feet long and in the shape of an L. From their position, the American soldiers could see the river and the road. The British were forced to use the road because it was surrounded by thick forest. In their fortification, the Americans waited with 22 cannons placed on the wall. Gates and the American troops were ready.

In September 1777, Gates was looking for an opportunity to prove to himself and Congress that he was a reliable leader for the Continental Army. Therefore, he decided to move the troops to a point where he knew the British Army would pass. Gates wanted a chance to fight. So, the Northern Continental Army headed to Saratoga, south of New York.

General Burgoyne and his troops continued their march without knowing what was waiting for them. Instead, he believed that General Howe's reinforcements were on their way. While the British were walking through a forest, they found a note pinned to a tree. It was a message from the rebels: "Don't go any further."

The American rebels knew they needed a different tactic to defeat the British. If they met them in an open field, the British had the advantage because that's how battles were fought during this time, and the British were better trained for that. That was the reason for Washington's defeat at Brooklyn Heights. Therefore, Gates and his men tried something new.

On September 19th, the American soldiers hid in the forest and fired at the British from cover when the British were out in the open. And so the battle began. By the afternoon, by using this hit-and-run tactic, the Americans retreated after causing 600 casualties to the British army.

After that victory, the Continental Army outnumbered the British troops. The revolutionaries felt confident, and Gates was sure they could defeat the enemy. However, there was about to be a big problem.

Another general in the Continental Army was also looking for his moment to shine. His name was Benedict Arnold. He had been on other missions but was never recognized. He thought his moment had come.

After the first victory in Saratoga, Gates met Arnold to discuss the following steps. Gates wanted to wait until the British attacked as their position was better to defend. Instead, Arnold suggested that they take advantage of the moment and hit the British again with a new offensive. However, the discussion turned into an argument, and Gates rejected Arnold's suggestions.

Unaware of the troubles on the rebels' side, the British general Burgoyne decided to take revenge, even though he already knew that no support was on the way. He prepared an attack on the south of Saratoga at a place called Bemis Heights.

On October 7th, Burgoyne made the first move and sent 1,500 men on a mission to learn about the American troops. Gates answered with 2,500 men who confronted them.

In the middle of the battle, General Arnold led an attack using men shooting from the woods. They climbed the trees and took position on the branches. They weren't using their uniforms and were invisible to the British. At his order, three American soldiers who had the British general on target fired and killed him.

After that, the British lost, and the Continental Army won. Even though it was under Arnold's leadership, Gates took the credit. This would be a problem later.

The British eventually retreated and abandoned their plan to take control of the Hudson Valley. The Continental Army's victory in Saratoga was another step towards independence.

THE WINTER AT VALLEY FORGE: SURVIVING THROUGH HARDSHIP

While General Gates won at Saratoga, things didn't go well for Washington in the South. Under Washington's command, the Continental Army was defeated in Pennsylvania. The Continental Congress had moved to York, and Philadelphia was then in British hands. Despite the victory at Saratoga, the situation was still difficult for the revolutionaries.

In December 1777, Washington retreated with the Continental Army, and once more, the troops had to march and endure the winter. They were cold, hungry, tired, and, worst of all, discouraged after the defeats they had suffered. Washington, however, wouldn't give up. The Continental Congress expected a successful military campaign in the spring to recover Philadelphia.

With that goal in mind, Washington led the Continental Army and set his camp in Valley Forge, a few miles away from occupied Philadelphia. Washington chose a place where they had easy access to water and wood, but they wouldn't easily find other necessary things to survive the winter. The living conditions in the valley were miserable. This time, the army was too weak to attempt a surprise attack as they did in New Jersey.

Despite the difficult conditions, Washington knew that he had only the winter to regroup the army and get ready again. The place he had chosen to settle the camp was strategic. It was close enough to keep an eye on the British troops and also had accessible farms to provide as many resources as possible. The camp was on the top of a hill surrounded by rivers. It was like a fort and made defending the Patriot Army's position easier.

The camp hosted about 12,000 soldiers and a smaller group of Native Americans and enslaved Africans who wanted to gain their own freedom. The soldiers weren't alone. Many wives and their children had joined the men and settled in Valley Forge as well. The Continental Army would turn the camp into a village.

Winter passed, and the Continental Army had a difficult time at Valley Forge. By February, 2,500 soldiers had died from disease, and many others were too weak to fight due to illnesses and hunger.

Washington realized that his troops weren't ready to fight and asked several times for support, money, and supplies. However, that kind of help never came. Instead, he received help from a Prussian(German) named Baron von Steuben. He helped Washington by providing the soldiers with military training.

The Continental Army also had the help of a French noble. His name was Gilbert du Motier, Marquis de Lafayette. He had joined Washington's army before the camp was settled in Valley Forge and participated in the battles. Even though he was French, he embraced the American cause and wanted to help the Patriots achieve independence.

Through Washington's strong and wise leadership and Von Steuben's training, the Continental Army recovered. By April 1778, the snow had melted. Washington had decided that the army wouldn't attempt a new attack until the summer, so the training and preparation continued during the spring.

THE SUMMER CAMPAIGN

Meanwhile, things were changing on the British side. Due to the catastrophic loss in Saratoga, Commander Howes was removed from his charge and replaced by General Clinton. He settled in Philadelphia, still under British control. In addition, the British had New York and its vital port and New Port, Rhode Island, on the northern extreme.

Even though the British had strengthened their presence on the shores, they knew the French were a threat. The French Navy could take any of those ports at any moment. Therefore, General Clinton received an order from King George to leave Philadelphia and focus his troops in New York. That way, they would be better prepared to resist if the French attacked.

The American Army had spies mixed among the British soldiers, and they told Washington that the British were leaving Philadelphia for New York. Washington made up his mind and decided to make a move. In June 1778, the 13,000 men that formed the Continental Army prepared to leave Valley Forge.

The revolutionary soldiers started a journey following the British, an army of about 12,000 men and a large caravan carrying all their military supplies. Both armies walked for weeks through New Jersey in the heat of the summer.

The Americans' strategy was to slow down the British march and make the path uneasy. Therefore, they pulled down trees to block roads, tore down bridges, and created skirmishes. Nonetheless, the British continued to advance. Washington outlined his plan.

On June 28th, a troop of 5,000 Continental soldiers led by Charles Lee stepped forward and tackled the British Army at the crossroads of Monmouth, even though they were outnumbered. They were going to attack the British rear. Meanwhile, Washington and the rest of the army would follow behind them. If the British attempted to retreat, they would let them go. If not, Washington would approach and join the battle with the 7,000 men who waited with him.

That morning of June was the beginning of the hottest day of that summer. Those soldiers who had suffered extreme temperatures in the winter were melting under a blazing sun. Their feet were burning, and they could barely carry their weapons.

They didn't have water to quench their thirst. The soldiers who had been suffering extremely cold temperatures in the winter were now melting under the blazing hot sun.

At noon, the two armies met face-to-face. The British did not retreat, and the smaller troop of 5,000 patriots started to panic under the weak leadership of Charles Lee, so Washington moved forward to engage in combat and rally the troops. The British were as tired as the Americans, and when they reached the battlefield, the Continental Army had already formed their ranks and stood in a stronger position. The training in Valley Forge was showing positive results. The militiamen had turned into a professional army.

The battle started around 1 o'clock in the afternoon and lasted for hours. Men from both sides fought bravely. Many of them died due to being shot. Many also died because of the extreme heat and their thirst. The British made several advances, but the Continental soldiers pushed them away time after time.

During the battle, an American woman named Mary Hays entered the battlefield, risking her life. She carried away the wounded and gave water to those who remained on the ground. The soldiers she helped later remembered her as Molly Pitcher.

The Battle of Monmouth was the largest of the Independence War. It lasted more than five hours. In the evening, the British general ordered the retreat and continued their march to New York. Washington counted it as a triumph.

Philadelphia was again under American control, and Benedict Arnold became the new governor.

Key Points

- After the Declaration of Independence, the British attacked the colonies.
- In the colonies, people had opposing opinions. The loyalists wanted to remain members of the British Empire and were loyal to King George III.
- The revolutionaries were determined to fight the independence war and drive out the British from the colonies.
- George Washington, Chief Commander of the Continental Army, settled a camp at Brooklyn Heights after forcing the British to escape from Boston.
- The British came back and attacked the Patriots. The Continental Army fled through the river during a foggy night.
- Washington retreated and settled with the Army in New Jersey. The British camp was on the other side of the Delaware River.
- Since the enemy didn't expect an attack during the winter, Washington led the Continental Army to cross the Delaware River during a snowstorm. They attacked the British in Trenton and obtained a new victory.
- Later, the British defeated Washington again and seized Philadelphia.
- The North Continental Army, led by General Gates, prepared to stop the British advance through New England. The Patriots fought the battle of Saratoga, and the independence war took a different course.
- Meanwhile, Washington prepared to attack the British and recover Philadelphia. He took the

Continental Army to Valley Forge, where they established a camp to spend the winter there. The soldiers were exhausted and demoralized.

- During the winter, a lot of soldiers died due to diseases and terrible living conditions. Nonetheless, Washington's leadership could keep the army together.
- Baron von Steuben came to help Washington. He was an experienced Prussian general and helped Washington turn a militia of Patriots into a professional army.
- A French noble called Marquis de Lafayette also joined the Continental Army.
- By the spring of 1778, the Continental Army was ready for the last attempt to defeat the Patriots, though it would take much longer.
- In the summer of 1778, the British left Philadelphia to concentrate their forces in New York.
- Washington confronted them with the renewed Continental Army. The two armies fought the Monmouth battle on June 28th. It was a triumph for the American Patriots.

CHAPTER 7
THE PATH TO VICTORY

Between 1778 and 1781, the Continental Army and the British Royal Army fought several battles, but neither was able to take a significant advantage over the rival. The British had lost most of their positions and resisted in some places on the coasts. Meanwhile, Great Britain engaged in armed conflicts with France and Spain in Europe. Therefore, King George didn't have enough resources to fight a war on two fronts.

On the other hand, the Continental Army was in better condition after the training received in Valley Forge, but the troops were exhausted. They had spent too much time far away from home, living in camps, eating poorly, and struggling with diseases. Both sides needed a good plan that could bring the conflict to an end. Both sides wanted a final victory.

Benjamin Franklin traveled to France searching for help for the rebels. Marquis de Lafayette, the military officer who volunteered to join the Continental Army, had returned to France and tried to persuade his King to support the American colonies. Soon, Lafayette would return to America, bringing good news.

France and Great Britain were old enemies, so getting French support for the colonies was possible. However, the French King only wanted to fight a war that could be won. After the events in 1777, the Continental Army's achievements let the French King know that the American Patriots were determined to win. The victory in Saratoga proved that the American rebels had a real opportunity of winning this war.

That encouraged the French King, Louis XVI, to enter the war and take sides with the enemy of his enemy. Soon, the French started sending supplies to assist the revolutionaries. The French participation was essential in the American Revolution. Since Louis XVI sent naval support, the British could no longer rely on their naval power and focus on the battles taking place on land. Now, the British had to fight on two fronts.

Washington knew he could count on this international support. By 1781, Washington also knew he needed a plan that could bring the Patriots an ultimate victory. He had two options: He could go to New York and hit the British Army there, where the North Continental Army had already won in Saratoga, or he could head south to Virginia. There, several troops of the army commanded by Comte de Grasse were ready to fight.

Almirante Comte de Grasse was French and came to America to provide naval support. He had decided to go to Virginia because the Chesapeake Bay was a better place to sail with his fleet. His choice eventually influenced Washington's decision.

By 1781, George Washington had moved his camp again. After several battles, he had led the Continental Army to Morristown, near New York. The British were in the north, also close to New York. The bulk of the British troops that were in Philadelphia had joined them. If the Continental Army attacked there, they would find strong resistance.

Therefore, Washington had more than one good reason to go south.

THE BATTLE OF YORKTOWN: THE FINAL SHOWDOWN

Like in the past, Washington, with his extraordinary leadership, moved the Continental Army through hundreds of miles. It was a difficult task. Soldiers were tired, and it was a long distance to cover marching and carrying all the military equipment. They had been at war for six years then. They were tired and poorly fed. Still, Washington was able to keep his men's spirits up.

Over 8,000 militia men moved from Morristown, New York, to Virginia. Other 12,000 men were waiting for them in the South. There, the French fleet had already joined the Continental Army.

The Continental Army was heading to Yorktown. The British settled there in the autumn of 1781 as the British General Cornwallis expected reinforcements. Meanwhile, his troops could rest and prepare again for battle. Nonetheless, about 20,000 men of the revolutionary forces moved toward Yorktown.

The British didn't expect the attack on Yorktown. Even though they had news of the French presence by sea, General Cornwallis believed Washington and his men were still in New York. He also hoped to receive more troops soon. However, he had already lost the support of the British Navy.

On September 5th, the French Navy attacked the British fleet. The Continental Army was still on its way to Yorktown. The French approached the harbor and opened fire on the British ships. The admirals of the royal navy tried to escape by sailing up, but the French intercepted them in Chesapeake.

This was the Battle of the Capes, and the British were defeated. They were forced to leave the coasts of Virginia, and the British troops stationed in Yorktown lost their naval support. And the French had free access to the shores. In just one battle, the French gained total control of the city harbor.

General Cornwallis felt trapped. He had lost his naval backup and had written several letters to General Clinton in New York asking for reinforcement. Although he received the promise of help back, it never arrived. Meanwhile, the Continental Army had closed all the roads, and the British had no escape.

The French had taken the city by the north, sailing through the York River. Washington and his troops settled in the South. The allied forces of France and the revolutionaries had surrounded the West. The British were locked in.

Again, Washington faced a new difficult decision: How would they defeat the British? His first idea was to launch a massive attack. Even though that would resolve the conflict quicker, it would mean too many casualties because the British were in an excellent position to defend themselves, and the city was surrounded by walls and soldiers.

The French Commander, General Rochambeau, proposed a siege and endless attack from the sea. On October 6th, the Continental soldiers begin the siege of Yorktown.

The Americans decided to dig trenches approaching the enemy lines in a parallel, zigzag formation, which were referred to as the parallels, to clear the way during a direct assault. The British, on their end, attempted to stop the building of the parallels. They opened fire on the Continental Army, trying to stop their laborers from digging. General Cornwallis still waited for reinforcements to come from New York. He thought that if he could resist until then, the British could win.

On the other hand, Washington knew he had to take the city before British military support came, so he didn't wait. The siege didn't only consist of surrounding the city and cutting off its supplies. There was constant fire from the French Navy cannonballs, and the Continental Army brought the trenches' lines closer and closer to the city.

Once the city was completely surrounded by the Patriots' trench line, Washington continued with the second stage of his plan. On October 14th, he launched a direct attack on the British troops. The operation began at night. In the middle of the night, the soldiers approached in complete silence. They didn't even charge their weapons to avoid being heard by the British. The operation was called Rochambeau, but the Americans called it instead, "Rush on boys!"

The attack began at 6:30 in the evening. A division of the Continental Army headed north of the city. They wanted the British to believe that they were going to attack the city at once. Lieutenant Colonel Alexander Hamilton led a group of 400 soldiers to start the attack. They climbed the walls of the forts and entered the city. Even though the British tried to defend themselves, Hamilton's men's attack was successful.

General Cornwallis's next letter to General Clinton was to tell him not to come to Yorktown, as the battle there had already been lost. There was no point in risking the rest of the army.

However, Clinton had already sailed towards the south, but his help wouldn't make it on time.

The British attempted a counterattack on October 15th but had no intent. The American troops had already entered the city, and the British had no resources to resist. On October 17th, the sound of a drum was heard in the midst of the smoke. A British soldier was standing alone and playing "parley." The British requested to negotiate the terms of surrender.

Another soldier extended a white handkerchief on top of a sword. This meant that the British had finally surrendered, and the Americans had won.

THE BRITISH'S LAST ATTEMPT

The final surrender of the British Army to the American Army took place outside of Yorktown on October 17th. The British requested honorable terms of surrender, but Washington didn't accept them. The British had denied it to the Americans in other battles after defeat. The British wanted to surrender and recognize the Patriots' victory if they would let them leave the city peacefully. Instead, Washington took them prisoners, including the general.

The Battle of Yorktown was the last major battle, as the British lacked the resources and money to raise another army. Still, the Revolutionary War wasn't over yet. It meant the end of hostilities, that is, the open combat on battlefields. However, the final deal had to be negotiated between Great Britain, the colonies, and the other nations involved in the war.

George Washington sent a message to the Continental Congress gathered in Philadelphia to inform them about the news: The Continental Army had beaten the South British

Army and taken 7,000 soldiers as prisoners, including General Cornwallis. The Patriots celebrated, but things were still far from being over. There were still groups of loyalists in Philadelphia who didn't support independence. However, they were a small minority.

Meanwhile, news crossed the Atlantic Ocean and reached France. There, Benjamin Franklin was still busy, engaged in diplomatic meetings. First, he had negotiated with the French Crown to obtain military assistance. Then, his next task was to lead the negotiation between Great Britain and the new state of America to declare peace.

France and Spain were involved in that stage as they supported the American rebels against Great Britain. To end the war, all the nations had to reach an agreement and sign peace.

King George and the British Parliament were the last to know about the events in America. On November 25th, the news arrived in England. Everybody was shocked. However, King George wasn't ready to give up a part of his empire so easily. He decided to make one more attempt to recover his colonies in North America. After all, the British still had parts of their army in New York and in the South.

In fact, war was still fought in South Carolina and Georgia, even after the triumph in Yorktown. There, the British were still strong. General Greene, George Washington's second in command, remained in the forests near Savannah and Charlestown, forcing the British to retreat to the cities. A lot of American lives were lost in this last part of the war.

However, back in London, King George lost all political support to continue the war. The Parliament decided to put an end to the war as it was very expensive and had taken too many

British lives. King George had no choice but to negotiate peace.

THE TREATY OF PARIS: A FORMAL GOODBYE TO BRITISH RULE

In April 1782, King George ordered the British commanders still in America to retreat their troops, bringing the war to an end on the battlefields. Meanwhile, peace negotiations began in Paris. These negotiations would shape the relationship between the British Crown and the new state, the United States.

Every war needs a peace treaty to consider it ended. All parties sign it, agreeing with that peace and the results. Sometimes, peace treaties say that one of the nations will lose territories or have to pay the winners. This time, the end of this war meant a lot more. As it was a war for independence. That meant it was fought by people who wanted freedom and to be a self-governed state. Therefore, this treaty of peace needed other nations, including Great Britain, to recognize this new state.

Benjamin Franklin was in Paris to handle the political negotiations to persuade the other European kingdoms to recognize a new free state in North America, which was the only way to secure their independence. John Jay, the current president of the Continental Congress, and John Adams also arrived to assist Franklin with this task.

After a long negotiation, the Treaty of Peace was finally signed on September 3rd, 1783, in Paris. The three American representatives wanted the other nations to recognize the United States as a free state. The other major objective of the negotiation was the establishment of the Western boundaries. After

Franklin, Jay, and Adams' involvement, it was accepted that the new state could expand its territory to the West.

The Treaty of Paris stated:

- The British Crown recognized New Hampshire, Massachusetts Bay, Rhode Island, Providence Plantations, Connecticut, New York, New Jersey, Pennsylvania, Delaware, Maryland, Virginia, North Carolina, South Carolina, and Georgia as the United States, a new and sovereign state. The colonial bond was broken forever.
- American people of the United States had full rights to use their natural resources.
- The citizens of the United States recovered all the properties taken in times of colonial power.
- There would be peace between the United States and Great Britain, and every prisoner on both sides was set free.

The United States was a free and sovereign nation, and peace was ensured.

Key Points

- Benjamin Franklin and the French Marquis de Lafayette made intense negotiations to gain the French King's support for the American rebel colonies. When the Continental Army won at Saratoga, Louis XVI agreed to send naval support.
- The French Navy headed South instead of New York.
- George Washington moved the Continental Army from New Jersey to Virginia to attack the British by

surprise, knowing the French Navy would meet them there.

- The British were in Yorktown, but most of the army had left Philadelphia and gathered in New York, where they expected the next attack.
- In September 1778, the French defeated the British Navy in Chesapeake Bay.
- The Continental Army sieged Yorktown and surrounded the defenseless British Army.
- On October 14th, the Continental Army crossed the fort's walls and successfully attacked the British.
- After a brief and weak resistance, the British surrendered.
- King George attempted a new operation to recover the lost colonies of his kingdom, but the Parliament didn't support his plan.
- Peace negotiations started in Paris, led by Benjamin Franklin, John Jay, and John Adams.
- The Patriots didn't only attempt to ensure peace. Great Britain and the other European nations had to recognize the United States as a free and sovereign nation.
- Negotiation was successful, and on September 3rd, 1783, the Treaty of Paris was signed. The United States was recognized by the world's free nations as a sovereign country. Independence and peace were ensured.

CHAPTER 8
THE BIRTH OF A NEW NATION

The Second Continental Congress approved the Declaration of Independence on July 4th, 1776. In 1783, the main European nations, including Great Britain, recognized the United States as a sovereign state with the signing of the Treaty of Paris.

While this meant the revolutionary process had ended, a new stage in our nation's history began. The Patriots that had accomplished the goal of independence now had the task of building a new nation.

What rights would the citizens have? Who would be considered a citizen? What would their laws be, and who would make these laws? These are just some of the many questions they had to answer.

They still had a lot of internal problems to solve. Not everybody in the colonies had agreed with the revolution. There were many British people still living in the new state and many others who had been loyalists, supporting the King and his power in America. What would happen to them? Unity was the first issue to address, and then the organization of the new state.

THE UNITED STATES CONSTITUTION: FRAMING A NEW GOVERNMENT

Almost seven years passed between the Declaration of Independence and the Treaty of Paris. During that time, the American colony-states no longer recognized British power. While the war for independence was being fought, and until peace was secured with the treaty, the Continental Congress was in charge of government in America.

A constitution gives a nation the legal frame that organizes every part of life. It decides the rights and responsibilities of the citizens, establishes who will be called a citizen, and defines what this actually means. A constitution also organizes the different offices within the government, such as Congress.

However, the process wasn't complete until the other nations of the world accepted the United States as a sovereign state. This means that the people of that state are in charge of their government, have the power to choose their own rules, trade with other nations, collect taxes, and declare war or peace without the involvement of any other power. That is only achieved when the other states recognize them.

The congressmen knew that any state needs a constitution. Therefore, in March 1781, they discussed and approved the Articles of Confederation. That became the first constitution of the United States. However, a new constitution was written in 1787 and approved in 1788. In 1789, Congress approved the final constitution. The 55 delegates of the Congress decided:

- The United States was a republic. Unlike a monarchy, the ruler in a republic is elected by popular vote and can stay only in power for a period of time. Power can't be passed on.
- The system adopted is a confederation. This means that each colony became a state with the right to have self-government and their own rules, but at the same time, recognize themselves as part of a greater organization: the Federal government.
- The Federal government was divided into three branches: legislative (the Congress), executive (the president), and judicial (the Supreme Court).
- In a republic, the government members must respect the law just as the rest of the population.

The Constitution had its first ten amendments in 1791, which added new articles to the original text. These amendments are called the Bill of Rights and establish the individual rights recognized and protected by the state.

The first president of the United States was elected by Congress after the approval of the Articles of Confederation in 1781. Even though they had declared independence, negotiations in Europe to sign the definitive peace were still ongoing. So, the Congress decided to name a temporary president. He was John Hanson.

The first elected president of the United States was George Washington. The election was through a group of delegates called the Electoral College. The delegates were, at the time, previously elected by the states. Washington obtained the total votes and took office on April 30th, 1789. His term ended in 1797.

The Congress, meanwhile, continued with the legislative responsibilities, and it did until the first delegates took office in 1789.

THE NEW LIFE AFTER INDEPENDENCE

The American Revolution started after the Sugar and Stamp Acts were passed by the British Parliament and ended when Great Britain and other European nations recognized the United States as a free nation through the Treaty of Paris. It was a long and difficult process that changed every person's life, even if they were not involved in the Revolutionary War. Sieged cities and popular militia brought the war close to everybody. Trading and other economic activities were interrupted, and the resources were saved for the army or to resist during the armed conflict.

The Declaration of Independence was an important action taken by the Continental Congress, but it didn't have a direct impact on the citizens. In fact, the Revolutionary War was just beginning, and it would continue for another seven years before The United States was actually free. After the war was over, a new stage started. Then, Patriots had to organize the government and how to ensure the survival of the citizens.

So, how did life change for American colonists when becoming free citizens of a new nation?

The truth is that social changes like those aren't noticeable from one moment to another. The political situation itself didn't automatically change after all the delegates gathered in Philadelphia voted and signed the Declaration of Independence. However, It did mean that the colonists weren't rebels breaking the empire's rules but people fighting for their liberty and self-government. Which was a huge difference. However, the process wasn't fully completed until the Treaty of Paris of 1783, which established that the other nations and The Empire actually recognized them as a nation and not as rebels.

American people didn't notice significant changes in their daily life straight away. After seven years of war, it took them a long time to recover their crops and animals, rebuild the cities and roads, and learn to live with their neighbors. It is important to remember that during the Revolutionary War, not all people supported the revolution cause. Many of them were loyalists, and many others were British living in America. It was a great challenge to build a country where people had different political ideas and still shared the territory.

In the free states, loyalists publicly disagreed with the new political situation. In New York, over 500 loyalists, including merchants, farmers, and enslaved people, signed a Declaration of Dependence reaffirming their loyalty to the King. The new nation had to develop tolerance and respect for everybody's rights, even those who didn't think in the same way.

There were many social groups that had to fight for many more years to ensure special rights. A few years after the approval of the Constitution, the Bill of Rights was added to include some of those rights in the Constitution. Religious freedom was one of the most important rights, especially for those who weren't Protestants.

Women also searched for more political rights. While everybody enjoyed civil rights, the possibility to vote and be a member of the government had to wait a while. Many women took part in the fight for independence, but politics was still limited for them.

Last but not least, slavery was another difficult issue to solve. Many enslaved people joined both sides during the Revolutionary War, expecting to gain their freedom. Even though many of those were freed, it was thanks to their masters' will or isolated resolutions. Slavery was still the main workforce after the Declaration of Independence and would be maintained for years.

THE IMPACT OF THE REVOLUTION: LOOKING AT THE LEGACY

The Declaration of Independence on July 4th, 1776, was indeed the most critical moment of the American Revolution. However, it was a process that took many years and passed through several different stages. It involved a lot of changes. It wasn't a simple shift in the government. Independence was the first step to building a new society, and it didn't happen in one day.

Similarly, the United States' independence didn't only affect the 13 former colonies. It represented a much more significant change. It is one of the most important revolutions in world history.

The American Revolution was a ground-breaking moment in the history of the American continent. It was the first political and social rebellion against the power of the European empires that ruled in America. Moreover, it was the first time people protested against the absolute power of the monarchy.

For the United States, it represents the first step to becoming a free nation. Although the influence of the American Revolution reached all of the American colonies, it even reached the European populations. The ideas and values that motivated the

American Patriots were also an inspiration to people from all over the world.

The United States of America chose to be a republic based on the ideas of democracy. This was also revolutionary. Most states of Europe were monarchies and empires. In a monarchy, political power is inherited, and people are subjects of the monarch. People don't have the possibility to vote for the ruler of their country. Great Britain did have a Parliament where delegates represented people's interests. However, that was the only way people could participate in their government.

In a republic, the law and the constitution are more important than any personal power of a king. In Great Britain, King George made his decisions with the support of the Parliament. However, in absolute monarchies, the King's power is more important than the laws in that country.

On the other hand, the American Revolution was based on democratic values that weren't so common at that time. The American colonies based their fight on the right of people to protest and rebel against injustice and to disobey rules that weren't good for them. Patriots claimed people have the right to openly express their ideas in the press, to gather and organize to search for the common good, and as a community, have the power to govern themselves.

The republican system and democratic values are the basis of most political systems in most countries today. It can be said that the American Revolution served as an example for people all over the world. It is a good thing for people to live in a republican democratic system because their rights are better protected, and they are free to express and act if their government makes decisions that don't benefit them.

The American Revolution was the first of a strong and long-lasting wave of revolutionary movements that spread across America and also some European countries. In America, it inspired all the colonial communities to break the colonial bond that kept them under the European kings' powers.

Until then, colonists didn't have any right to participate in the local governments, weren't considered citizens, and couldn't decide on their resources. Even if their families had come as settlers to work for the Crown, people born in America didn't have the same rights as European citizens.

After the American Revolution, Americans from the Spanish and French colonies also organized themselves to take control of their own nations. In Haiti, a French colony, the enslaved population started a revolution in 1791 and achieved independence in 1803. In Río de la Plata (today known as Argentina, Uruguay, Chile, Bolivia, and Paraguay) and Mexico, both Spanish colonies, the revolutionary process started in 1810.

From then on, all of the American colonies searched and achieved independence and became free sovereign states. After they declared independence, the United States was the first to recognize them as free states in the world. The citizens of the United States knew the importance of liberty and self-governance. All of those new countries and Patriots of all America recognized the influence of the American Revolution.

After gaining independence, many of those new American countries used the Constitution of the United States as an example to create their own laws. That is one of the reasons why the new American countries became republics instead of monarchies, as there were in Europe.

However, it was not only the Americans who felt that they needed to fight against the abuse of absolute power by the monarchs. Many European intellectuals and philosophers came to the United States to see how these young nations had overcome all the obstacles and dared to install a modern republic system. They went back to Europe and developed new theories about republicanism and democracy.

The American Revolution also had an influence on the French Revolution. The French Revolution was another political process of political changes that represented the beginning of a new era for the French.

The Revolutionary War in America was one of the first things that started the French Revolution. The French King Louis XVI agreed to create an alliance with the American colonies and support them in gaining independence. The King saw it as a chance to weaken one of his greatest enemies, Great Britain.

However, the French people didn't accept this. The French nation was suffering from a very difficult financial situation, and the King spent all of the money on a foreign war. France's involvement in a war in America made people angrier with the King. And this wasn't all.

People like Marquis de Lafayette were actually in America during the Revolutionary War and were truly inspired by the Americans standing up for their rights, opposing oppression, and fighting for their freedom. Lafayette had been with George Washington and the Continental Army in Valley Forge. Lafayette helped Washington train the revolutionary army and taught him how to encourage people to fight.

Even though Lafayette belonged to a privileged class in France, he returned with revolutionary ideas. He was one of the nobles who stood up for the people and promoted a change in the French absolute monarchy.

Key Points

- After the Declaration of Independence, a lot of things had to be fixed.
- The government was in charge of the Congress until, in 1781, the delegates approved the Articles of Confederation and declared John Hanson as provisional president.
- When other nations recognized the United States as a peer, the new state moved forward to organize itself.
- In 1789, the United States had the first constitution that established the new government. The political system was a republic and a confederation.
- Each colony became free states that recognized themselves as members of a confederation with a federal administration.
- The power was organized into three branches: legislative, executive, and judicial.
- In 1789, the United States had its first Congress with representatives elected by popular vote and its first president. George Washington took office after being elected by the Electoral College by unanimous vote.
- The Declaration of Independence was an important step in changing the political system, but the changes didn't immediately affect everybody's daily lives.
- Many people were loyalists even after the Declaration of Independence and also had the right to express their ideas.
- Civil rights like freedom of speech and religious freedom were equally achieved by men and women.

However, other political rights, such as voting or becoming a public officer, took longer for women to achieve.

- Even though enslaved people participated in the Revolutionary War, and many achieved freedom, slavery remained for several years after independence.
- The American Revolution was a critical moment in mankind's history.
- It inspired people from all over the world to oppose the tyranny of absolute monarchs.
- After the American Revolution, most American countries started their own revolutionary process and declared independence. That was the end of colonialism in America, although there are still a few colonies on the continent.
- The American Revolution inspired and was one of the triggers of the French Revolution.
- The American Revolution and the Constitution of the United States were an example for nations all over the world. The United States was the first to adopt a republican system and embrace democratic principles. Today, most states consider them the best option to ensure respect and attention to the individual's rights and the best way to secure people's involvement in the political system.

TIMELINE

THE MOST IMPORTANT EVENTS DURING THE AMERICAN REVOLUTION

1754-1763: The French and Indian War

1764: The Sugar Act

1765: The Stamp Act

1767: The Townshend Acts

1768: The British troops occupy Boston

1770, March 5th: Boston Massacre

1773, December 16th: Boston Tea Party

1774, March-June: Coercive Acts, named Intolerable Acts by the rebel colonists

1774, September 5th - October 26th: First Continental Congress

1775, April 19th: War breaks out in Lexington and Concord

1775, April: Boston siege begins

1775, May 5th: Second Continental Congress

1775, June 17th: Battle of Bunker Hill

1776, January: Thomas Paine publishes *Common Sense*

1776, July 4th: Declaration of Independence by the Second Continental Congress

1776, December: Washington and the Continental Army cross the Delaware River

1777, October 17th: Battle of Saratoga

1778-1779: Washington and the Continental Army spent the winter at Valley Forge

1781: Siege and Battle of Yorktown

1783: Treaty of Paris

FUN ACTIVITIES
GET CREATIVE WITH HISTORY

Match the Delegate with the Correct Colony

You read about all these patriots in this book. Do you remember which colony they represented during the American Revolution? Hint: You can match more than one name to some colonies. You might not need some of the colonies.

George Washington	New Hampshire
John Jay	Virginia
John Adams	Pennsylvania
Samuel Adams	Rhode Island
John Dickinson	Georgia
Benjamin Franklin	Massachusetts
Thomas Jefferson	New York

Complete the Paragraphs with One of the Words

Here, you have to read carefully and complete the blank spaces with the words in the list. You won't need to repeat any of them.

The Boston Massacre   Loyalists   Battle

Boston Tea Party   Lexington   Bunker Hill

Siege   Patriot

1. The _____ is the name given to the protest of the colonists that threw a British tea shipment into the sea.
2. Those who didn't oppose the British King's power were called _____.
3. The _____ of Saratoga resulted in a victory for the Continental Army.
4. The Continental Army built a fort at _____ and caused several casualties to the British in June 1775.
5. It was called _____ when British soldiers opened fire on a crowd and killed five colonists.
6. Due to the Boston _____, the British army had to evacuate to New York.
7. Paul Revere warned the _____ of Massachusetts to be prepared as the British troops were coming.
8. The Revolutionary War started with the confrontations at _____ and Concord.

What Happened First?

This time, you have to choose the event that happened first.

What happened first:

... the Battle of Saratoga or the Declaration of Independence?

... the Boston Massacre or the Intolerable Acts?

... the Sugar Act or the French and Indian War?

... Washington crossed the Delaware River or the Boston Siege?

... the Treaty of Paris or the Battle of Yorktown?

Quiz Time: How Much Do You Remember?

1. Who were the first Europeans that arrived in America in 1492?

    a. The Portuguese
    b. The Spanish
    c. The British
    d. The Dutch

2. Who was the King or queen of England when Great Britain had its first colony in North America?

    a. George III
    b. Louis XV
    c. Louis XVI
    d. Elizabeth I

3. Which of the following was the last colony settled by the British in North America?

    a. Virginia
    b. Georgia
    c. Pennsylvania
    d. Maryland

4. Which of the following current states of the United States isn't one of the former colonies?

    a. New York

b. Louisiana

c. Rhode Island

d. New Hampshire

5. What was the name of the first British colonists' settlement in North America?

a. Plymouth

b. Maryland

c. Jamestown

d. Georgetown

6. Who were the settlers that came from Great Britain on the ship called Mayflower in 1620?

a. Puritans running away from religious persecution.

b. Irish escaping from the British government.

c. Christopher Columbus' crew.

d. People hired by the Virginia Company who searched for commercial bonds in America.

7. What were the colonists' major problems in the early years of the colonies?

a. Unknown diseases

b. Native American people's attacks

c. Shortage of resources to survive

d. All of them

8. Which of the following business allowed the early colonists to earn a lot of money?

a. Growing and selling living cattle

b. Growing and selling tobacco

c. Making machinery for the factories

d. Trading wool

9. What did John Dickinson do in his hometown in Delaware?

a. He was a sailor

b. He was a farmer and later a politician

c. He was a lawyer

d. He was a soldier

10. John Jay and John Adams both had the same professional activity. What were they?

a. Farmers

b. Businessmen

c. Lawyers

d. Soldiers

11. Samuel Adams had two jobs before becoming a politician. First, he tried to run his own business and failed. Which was his other job?

a. Police officer

b. Landowner

c. Judge

d. Tax collector

12. When the French settled in the territories claimed by the British, Virginia's colonial government sent a colonel in charge of the militia to persuade them to leave. Who was he?

a. George Washington

b. Benedict Arnold

c. Paul Revere

d. Horatio Gates

13. After the Seven Year's War, the British Parliament passed the Sugar Act and the Stamp Act. What were the reasons for adding a new tax to the colonists?

a. The King was upset with the colonists for starting the war.

b. The British Crown needed money because the war was very expensive.

c. The British Parliament wanted to punish the rebel colonists.

d. The King started a new military campaign to conquer Canada.

14. Which of the following statements is true about the Boston Massacre?

a. It happened under the Liberty Tree.

b. The Sons of Liberty shot and killed five British soldiers.

c. The British soldiers shot and killed five colonial citizens.

d. The Liberty Tree was cut down.

15. Why did the colonists carry out the Boston Tea Party?

a. To protest against the Seven Years' War.

b. To start the Revolutionary War.

c. To protest against the new taxes on tea and goods.

d. To support the Declaration of Independence.

16. Who was the woman credited for having made the first American flag?

a. Abigail Adams
b. Betsy Ross
c. Mercy Otis Warren
d. Margaret Corbin

17. A lot of women played a key role during the American Revolution. What did Molly Pitcher that made her one of the dearest heroines in our history?

a. She took her husband's place on the battlefield in Yorktown.
b. She was a delegate from Virginia in the First Continental Congress.
d. She was an American spy working behind the enemy line.
e. She helped the wounded on the battlefield at Monmouth.

18. The Second Continental Congress chose one of the delegates to write the first draft of the Declaration of Independence. It was later reviewed, but who wrote that first manuscript?

a. Benjamin Franklin
b. George Washington
c. Thomas Jefferson
d. Alexander Hamilton

19. The "shot heard around the world" is considered the moment of the beginning of the Revolutionary War. Where did the incident happen?

    a. At Lexington and Concord
    b. At Bunker Hill
    c. At Saratoga
    d. At Yorktown

20. The American Revolution was achieved thanks to the efforts and commitment of many men and women. However, some of those men are considered the Founding Fathers of our nation for their unique contributions to independence. Which of the following isn't considered a Founding Father?

    a. Benedict Arnold
    b. George Washington
    c. Benjamin Franklin
    d. John Jay

21. Which strategy was developed by the North Continental Army at Saratoga to defeat the British troops?

    a. They sieged New York.
    b. They crossed the Delaware River in the middle of the winter when nobody expected it.
    c. The soldiers hid in the forest and attacked the British Army when they passed by.
    d. They used the French naval support to bombard New York.

22. By the end of 1777, the British had taken Philadelphia, and George Washington needed a plan to ensure victory. He settled his camp at Valley Forge. What happened after that?

a. George Washington and the Continental Army sieged Boston.
b. The American Patriots had a decisive victory in the Battle of Monmouth.
c. Paul Revere warned the Minutemen in Lexington and Concord.
d. Benedict Arnold led the Continental Army to defeat and push the British out of Philadelphia.

23. The Battle of Yorktown was the final strike of the American Revolution and the end of combats in the Revolutionary War. What happened there?

a. The British in Yorktown didn't get reinforcement and surrendered to the Continental Army.
b. George Washington decided to leave Yorktown and attack New York.
c. The French navy concentrated in New York and attacked the city.
d. The British were defeated in Yorktown, New York, and Georgia.

24. When and how did the Revolutionary War formally finish?

a. When the British requested to parley outside Yorktown on October 15th, 1781.
b. When the British evacuated Philadelphia in 1778.
c. When the United States of America signed the Treaty of Paris on September 3rd, 1783.

d. When the Second Continental Congress approved the Declaration of Independence on July 4th, 1776.

25. Why was the Treaty of Paris so important?

a. Because after that, all the British that lived in America left and moved to Great Britain.
b. Because it ended the war, and the rest of the nations recognized the United States as a free nation.
c. Because it allowed Congress to approve a constitution.
d. Because Benjamin Franklin finally finished his job in Europe.

ANSWERS SHEET

Match the Delegate with the Correct Colony

George Washington - Virginia

John Jay - New York

John Adams - Massachusetts

Samuel Adams - Massachusetts

John Dickinson - Pennsylvania

Benjamin Franklin - Pennsylvania

Thomas Jefferson - Virginia

Complete the Paragraphs with One of the Words

The **Boston Tea Party** is the name given to the protest of the colonists that threw a British tea shipment to the sea.

Those who didn't oppose the British King's power were called **loyalists**.

The **battle** of Saratoga resulted in a victory for the Continental Army.

The Continental Army built a fort at **Bunker Hill** and caused several casualties to the British in June 1775.

It was called **the Boston Massacre** when British soldiers opened fire on a crowd and killed five colonists.

Due to the Boston **siege**, the British army had to evacuate to New York.

Paul Revere warned the **Patriots** of Massachusetts to be prepared as the British troops were coming.

The Revolutionary War started with the confrontations at **Lexington** and Concord.

What Happened First?

What happened first was

... the Declaration of Independence.

... the Boston Massacre.

... the French and Indian War.

... the Boston Siege.

... the Battle of Yorktown.

Quiz Correct Answers

1. b. The Spanish
2. d. Elizabeth I
3. b. Georgia
4. b. Louisiana
5. c. Jamestown
6. a. Puritans running away from religious persecution
7. d. All of them
8. b. Growing and selling tobacco

9. b. He was a farmer and later a politician
10. c. Lawyers
11. d. Tax collector
12. a. George Washington
13. b. The British Crown needed money because the war was very expensive
14. c. The British soldiers shot and killed five colonial citizens
15. c. To protest against the new taxes on tea and goods
16. b. Betsy Ross
17. d. She helped the wounded on the battlefield at Monmouth
18. c. Thomas Jefferson
19. a. At Lexington and Concord
20. a. Benedict Arnold
21. c. The soldiers hid in the forest and attacked the British Army when they passed by
22. b. The American Patriots had a decisive victory in the Battle of Monmouth
23. a. The British in Yorktown didn't get reinforcement and surrendered to the Continental Army
24. c. When the United States of America signed the Treaty of Paris on September 3rd, 1783
25. b. Because it ended the war, and the rest of the nations recognized the United States as a free nation

CONCLUSION

Most people think that history is about dates and facts. Instead, history is about people's lives. The nation we live in today is a result of the hard work and courage of those who lived before us. Learning about these people's lives is the best way to learn about history.

The American Revolution was a milestone in our nation's history, of America as a continent, and of the world. It brought a message of peace, freedom, and courage to stand up for individuals' rights. Who we are now is what revolutionaries dreamed and fought for.

Throughout these pages, we have seen that some names are better remembered than others. Some men and women had an outstanding role in the development of our country's history. They deserve a special place in our memory.

However, we shall not forget all the other unknown people who made their smaller but invaluable contributions. The history of the United States of America started a long time ago before it was even called that. Our country was built by the hands of the first settlers who faced the dangers of the unknown and by all those who later fought for the colonists' rights.

The path to freedom was long and full of obstacles. Nonetheless, determination and ideals led the Patriots to victory. The Revolutionary War was fought on the battlefields but also in the houses, on the streets, and in the meeting chambers. Our nation was born from the heat of battle and the lightning of the new understanding of human dignity.

The thrilling history of the American Revolution teaches us that freedom and democracy were built at a high cost. Common people like us had to leave their daily lives to become soldiers. Many of them risked everything they had to fight for a greater purpose than personal growth. The American Revolution was the beginning of our nation's history but also one of the most important events in the history of humankind.

Now, it is our turn to honor them and commit to doing our part: We will cherish, protect, and preserve liberty and democracy. We must all take care of this priceless legacy.

GLOSSARY

Act: It refers to an Act of the British Parliament. It is a new rule that is created and approved by the members of the Parliament, and the king or queen has given it their consent.

Assembly: It is a gathering of people with a particular purpose. When talking about an assembly for political purposes, it means that representatives of the population or social groups meet and discuss to make decisions approved by all or the majority of them.

Boycott: It is a means of protest or a way to punish by stopping commercial relationships. If a nation stops buying or selling goods from another, it will cause economic damage.

Civil rights: Those are the rights of every human being acquired just by being born and must be respected and protected by the government. Civil rights imply that every person must have equal opportunities and be equally treated under the law regardless of any personal characteristic. The right to free speech and press, liberty, religious freedom, and to work and run a business are some of the most important.

Colony: It is a piece of land conquered and occupied by a country beyond its borders. This territory is populated and remains under the power of the conquering country. A colony doesn't have self-government. The colonists don't have the power to choose their own government or give themselves rules.

Congress: It is a formal assembly with a particular purpose. In modern political systems, the Congress is the institution in charge of the legislative branch of the government. Representatives of the states from different political parties discuss and create the laws.

Conservative: It is a political ideology that attempts to preserve the ideas and ways to do things as they already are, with minor changes. During the American Revolution, the conservatives were the loyalists who didn't want to break up the bond with the British Crown.

Delegate: It is a person who is elected by different means to represent a district or group of people in an assembly or Congress. They have the mission to express the opinions of the group they represent and vote on behalf of them.

Democracy: It is a political system based on the participation of the population in the government. The members of the government are elected by popular vote and hold their office positions for established terms. The power belongs ultimately to the people, though it is exerted by the representatives chosen by the population through regular elections.

Empire: It is a state or country that has annexed or conquered other countries and territories beyond the original borders. It is ruled by a monarch called an emperor. The main difference between a kingdom and an empire is that the latter searched to expand their territories by conquests.

Fort: It is a place built with the purpose of providing military protection. It usually consists of walls, barracks, and guard posts.

Freedom: It is the possibility to act, think, and express without any coercion to do or not to do it. In the context of the American Revolution, freedom implied that the colonies could be self-governing without the British Crown's coercion through Acts or military intervention.

Harbor: The ports where the commercial and military ships arrived and departed. They were very important as ships could reach them with supplies and military reinforcement.

Independence: It is a condition in which the subject is not linked and subordinated to any other entity. In the context of the American Revolution, the colonies weren't independent as they were under British power. Independence meant the break of that subordination link to have their own government, create their own rules, and control their economy.

Indian War: The war unleashed in 1754 in North America was known as the French and the Indian War. It started when the French attempted to colonize the lands near the British colonies. The conflict involved Native American people who also lived there.

Loyalists: Colonists that remained loyal to the British king after the Revolutionary War started. They opposed the revolutionaries.

Monarchy: It is a political system where all the power is held by one person, the king or queen. The ruler holds the power until they die or abdicate (resigns to power) and is not achieved through popular election. Instead, it is inherited.

Nation: A community of people that share particular characteristics such as a language, a territory, and a common history. Nationalists consider themselves as members of the nation. The word is also used to define a group of people living in a territory under a common government.

Parliament: It is (and was in times of the American Revolution) the legislative branch of the government. It is the assembly in charge of discussing and creating the laws for Great Britain and all the territories under the imperial power.

Patriot: It refers to a person who fights for the rights and freedom of their country and people. In the context of the American Revolution, the Patriots were those who opposed the British acts that were against the colonists' rights and later joined or supported the Continental Army.

Pilgrim: It is the name given to a person that migrates or moves to other lands due to religious reasons. In America, the Pilgrims were the Puritans that fled from Great Britain in 1620 to escape religious persecution and migrated to the British lands in America on the Mayflower. They settled at Plymouth.

Puritans: They were practitioners of a branch of Protestantism in Great Britain and New England. Protestantism was a new religion that resulted from the Protestant Reformation that took place in Germany and other parts of Europe in the 1400s and 1500s. They share most Christian beliefs with Catholicism but don't recognize the authority of the Pope.

Radical: It is a person who proposes drastic changes to the existing conditions. In the context of the American Revolution, radicals like Thomas Jefferson spoke about independence while the rest of the colonists were still searching for a reconciliation with the British king.

Rebellion: It is an open and armed manifestation against the ruling power. It is usually poorly organized. It is usually vanquished or controlled by the authorities.

Redcoats: It was the name given by the revolutionaries to the British soldiers of the royal army. It referred to the color of their uniforms. The Continental soldiers had blue uniforms to distinguish them from the enemy.

Revolution: It is a sudden and massive upheaval to attempt to change radically the current social and political conditions. It is usually armed and implies the development of organized groups that act for a prolonged period of time, seeking to achieve their goals.

Siege: It is a military action that surrounds a city, town, or garrison by building walls, trenches, or military camps. The objective is to prevent the sieged place from receiving supplies and force rendition. It usually involves persistent fire attacks.

Sovereignty: It is the faculty of a state to rule without any further intermission. It means that a sovereign state has a government chosen and elected on its own and has the power and capacity to provide its rules and manage its economic resources. There isn't any other political power above the sovereignty of a state.

State: It is a politically organized community living in a given territory with certain geographical and legal borders, and a formal government. States are recognized as sovereign political units by the other existing states in the global political system.

Tax: It is a charge imposed on people or businesses by a competent public authority. It is in exchange for public services such as organization or security.

REFERENCES

Abigail Adams (1744 - 1818). (2015, July 25). National Park Service. https://www.nps.gov/adam/learn/historyculture/abigail-adams-1744-1818.htm

Alexander Hamilton. (n.d.). Mount Vernon. https://www.mountvernon.org/library/digitalhistory/digital-encyclopedia/article/alexander-hamilton/#:~:text=Courtesy% 20National% 20Gallery% 20of% 20Art,of% 20the% 20American% 20financial% 20system

American Revolution Facts. (n.d.). American Battlefield Trust. https://www.battlefields.org/learn/articles/american-revolution-faqs

Atkinson, R. (n.d.). *Continental Army.* Mount Vernon. https://www.mountvernon.org/library/digitalhistory/digital-encyclopedia/article/continental-army/

Battle of Monmouth. (n.d.). Mount Vernon. https://www.mountvernon.org/library/digitalhistory/digital-encyclopedia/article/battle-of-monmouth/

Battle of Yorktown in the American Revolution. (n.d.). American Battlefield Trust. https://www.battlefields.org/learn/revolutionary-war/battles/yorktown

Benjamin Franklin - One of America's Founding Fathers. (2020, June 11). The Constitutional Walking Tour.

Big Idea 8: After the Declaration: What Happens Next? (n.d.). Museum of the American Revolution. https://www.amrevmuseum.org/big-idea-8-after-the-declaration-what-happens-next

Big Idea 3: Soldiers of the Revolutionary War. (n.d.). Museum of the American Revolution. https://www.amrevmuseum.org/big-idea-3-soldiers-of-the-revolutionary-war

Boston Tea Party Ships & Museum. (n.d.). *American Revolution history & time of the Revolutionary War.* https://www.bostonteapartyship.com/american-revolution

Bunker Hill Battle facts and summary. (n.d.). American Battlefield Trust. https://www.battlefields.org/learn/revolutionary-war/battles/bunker-hill

Cashin, E. (2020, September 30). *Revolutionary War in Georgia.* New Georgia Encyclopedia. https://www.georgiaencyclopedia.org/articles/history-archaeology/revolutionary-war-in-georgia/

Colonial and Early American New York (2017, May 14). National Park Service. https://www.nps.gov/stli/learn/historyculture/places_colonial_early_american.htm

REFERENCES

Colonists respond with boycott. (n.d.). Historycentral. https://www.historycentral.com/Revolt/Boycott.html

Computer Fan. (2012, August 3). *King George's response to the Olive Branch Petition read by John Hancock.* [Video] YouTube. https://www.youtube.com/watch?v=5JTxVHQAp8w&list=RDLVkhqq1dt3BuM&start_radio=1

Constitution of the United States. (n.d.). Senate.gov. https://www.senate.gov/about/origins-foundations/senate-and-constitution/constitution.htm

D'Entremont, J. (n.d.). *Maritime Commerce, Maritime History of Massachusetts.* National Park Service. https://www.nps.gov/nr/travel/maritime/commerce.htm

De Bry, T. & Bacon N. (n.d.). *Timeline: Colonization and settlement, 1585–1763.* Gilder Lehrman Institute of American History. https://www.gilderlehrman.org/history-resources/online-exhibitions/timeline-colonization-and-settlement-1585-1763

Declaration of Independence: A Transcription. (2023, January 31). National Archives. https://www.archives.gov/founding-docs/declaration-transcript

Duplessis, J.S. (n.d.). *Benjamin Franklin.* Mount Vernon. https://www.mountvernon.org/library/digitalhistory/digital-encyclopedia/article/benjamin-franklin/

Encyclopedia Britannica. (2022, October 20). *Sugar Act.* https://www.britannica.com/money/topic/Sugar-Act

Encyclopedia Britannica. (2023, June 14). *Stamp Act.* https://www.britannica.com/event/Stamp-Act-Great-Britain-1765

Encyclopedia Britannica. (2023, July 3). *Continental Congress.* https://www.britannica.com/topic/Continental-Congress

Encyclopedia Britannica. (2023, July 4). *Samuel Adams.* https://www.britannica.com/biography/Samuel-Adams

Eugène, P. & Prévost, B.L. (n.d.). *Battle of Saratoga.* Mount Vernon. https://www.mountvernon.org/library/digitalhistory/digital-encyclopedia/article/battle-of-saratoga/#:~:text=The% 20battle% 20of% 20Saratoga% 20took,rest% 20of% 20the% 20United% 20States

European Colonization of North America. (n.d.). National Geographic Society. https://education.nationalgeographic.org/resource/european-colonization-north-america/

First Continental Congress. (n.d.). Mount Vernon. https://www.mountvernon.org/library/digitalhistory/digital-encyclopedia/article/first-continental-congress/#:~:text=The% 20First% 20Continental% 20Congress% 20convened,future% 20under% 20growing% 20British% 20aggression

Getchell, M. (n.d.). *The Boston Tea Party.* Khan Academy. https://www.khanacademy.org/humanities/us-history/road-to-revolution/the-american-revolution/a/the-boston-tea-party

Getchell, M. (n.d.). *The Second Continental Congress*. Khan Academy. https://www.khanacademy.org/humanities/us-history/road-to-revolution/the-american-revolution/a/the-second-continental-congress#:~:text=There% 20were% 20two% 20main% 20factions,and% 20Thomas% 20Jefferson% 20of% 20Virginia

Hand, T. (2023, February 22). *Thomas Paine's Common Sense inspires a nation*. Americana Corner. https://www.americanacorner.com/blog/paine-common-sense

How did the English Colonize America? (2021, April 26). Knowledgia. [Video]. YouTube. https://www.youtube.com/watch?v=H2Gl4QFA6mA

History. (2022, October 20). Declaring American Independence | The Revolution (E3) | Full Episode. [Video]. YouTube. https://www.youtube.com/watch?v=Mxrl2FzzQqk

History. (2022, October 27). Washington's daring gamble to save America | The Revolution (S1, E4) | Full Episode. [Video]. YouTube. https://www.youtube.com/watch?v=VibTps6VRJg

History. (2022, November 3). The American Revolution leads to a world war | The Revolution (S1, E5) | Full Episode. [Video]. YouTube. https://www.youtube.com/watch?v=0Ynz22y6jsk

History. (2022, November 10). George Washington forges his army | The Revolution (S1, E6) | Full Episode. [Video]. YouTube. https://www.youtube.com/watch?v=qWsi_LqPePo

History. (2022, December 15). The US victory at Yorktown births a nation | The Revolution (S1, E11) | Full Episode. [Video]. YouTube. https://www.youtube.com/watch?v=ZBWN9Bdg3l4

Isaacson, W. (2003, July 31). *Benjamin Franklin joins the revolution*. Smithsonian Magazine. https://www.smithsonianmag.com/history/benjamin-franklin-joins-the-revolution-87199988/

Italie, H. (2015, July 4). *What you should know about forgotten founding father John Jay*. Associated Press. PBS. https://www.pbs.org/newshour/nation/forgotten-founding-father

James Madison. (n.d.). The White House. https://www.whitehouse.gov/about-the-white-house/presidents/james-madison/#:~:text=James% 20Madison% 2C% 20America% 27s% 20fourth% 20President,% E2% 80% 9CFather% 20of% 20the% 20Constitution.% E2% 80% 9D

Jamestown Colony. (2020, February 18). Revolutionary-War.net. https://www.revolutionary-war.net/jamestown-colony/

John Dickinson. (n.d.). Delaware Division of Historical and Cultural Affairs. https://history.delaware.gov/john-dickinson-plantation/dickinsonletters/john-dickinson/

Kerri, L.A. (n.d.). *Biography: Betsy Ross*. National Women's History Museum. https://www.womenshistory.org/education-resources/biographies/betsy-

REFERENCES

ross#:~:text=Considered% 20essential% 20to% 20the% 20Ameri-
can,George% 20Washington% 20finish% 20the% 20design

Lewis, R. (2023, April 12). *Plymouth Rock*. Encyclopedia Britannica.
https://www.britannica.com/topic/Plymouth-Rock-United-States-history

Lexington and Concord: The Shot Heard 'Round the World. (n.d.). American
Battlefield Trust. https://www.battlefields.org/learn/articles/lexington-and-
concord-shot-heard-round-world

Library of the Congress. (n.d.). *Overview | The American Revolution, 1763 -
1783*. https://www.loc.gov/classroom-materials/united-states-history-
primary-source-timeline/american-revolution-1763-1783/overview/

Library of the Congress. (n.d.). The English establish a foothold at Jamestown,
1606-1610 | Colonial settlement, 1600s - 1763. https://www.loc.gov/class-
room-materials/united-states-history-primary-source-timeline/colonial-
settlement-1600-1763/english-at-jamestown-1606-1610/

Maloy, M. (n.d.). *The Boston Liberty Tree*. American Battlefield Trust.
https://www.battlefields.org/learn/articles/boston-liberty-tree

Mayflower and Mayflower Compact. (n.d.). Plimoth Patuxet Museums.
https://plimoth.org/for-students/homework-help/mayflower-and-
mayflower-compact

Meade, R. (2023, July 14). *Patrick Henry*. Encyclopedia Britannica.
https://www.britannica.com/biography/Patrick-Henry

Mercy Otis Warren (1728-1814). (2020, May 11). Mount Vernon.
https://www.mountvernon.org/library/digitalhistory/digital-encyclope-
dia/article/mercy-otis-warren-1728-1814/

Milestones: 1750-1775. French and Indian War/Seven Years' War, 1754–63.
(n.d.). Office of the Historian. https://history.state.gov/milestones/1750-
1775/french-indian-war

*Milestones: 1750-1775. Incidents leading up to the French and Indian War,
1753–54* (n.d.). Office of the Historian. https://history.state.gov/mile-
stones/1750-1775/incidents

Milestones: 1776–1783. Continental Congress, 1774–1781. (n.d.). Office of the
Historian. https://history.state.gov/milestones/1776-1783/continental-
congress

Milestones: 1776–1783. The Declaration of Independence, 1776. (n.d.). Office
of the Historian. https://history.state.gov/milestones/1776-1783/declara-
tion#:~:text=By% 20issuing% 20the% 20Declaration% 20of,colonists% 27%
20motivations% 20for% 20seeking% 20independence

Monmouth Battle Facts and Summary. (n.d.). American Battlefield Trust.
https://www.battlefields.org/learn/revolutionary-war/battles/monmouth

Moran, P. (2023, January 13). *The Battle of Bunker Hill (US)*. National Park
Service. https://www.nps.gov/articles/000/the-battle-of-bunker-hill.htm

Mr. Strauch's Podcast. (2017, June 15). *July 2nd, 1776 - The vote for indepen-*

dence. [Video]. YouTube. https://www.youtube.com/watch?v=vFPFhu-OsvQ4&list=RDLVkhqq1dt3BuM&index=3

On this day: The First Continental Congress concludes. (2022, October 26). The National Constitution Center. https://constitutioncenter.org/blog/on-this-day-the-first-continental-congress-concludes

Orrison, R. (2021, April 30). Militia, Minutemen, and Continentals: The American Military Force in the American Revolution. American Battlefield Trust. https://www.battlefields.org/learn/articles/militia-minutemen-and-continentals-american-military-force-american-revolution

OverSimplified. (2018, August 30). The American Revolution (Part 1). [Video] YouTube. https://www.youtube.com/watch?v=rtYC2jx1LMo&t=594s

Patrick Henry. (n.d.). American Battlefield Trust. https://www.battlefields.org/learn/biographies/patrick-henry

Paul Revere - The Midnight Ride. (n.d.). Paul Revere House. https://www.paulreverehouse.org/the-real-story/

Portrait of Benjamin Franklin. (n.d.). American Battlefield Trust. https://www.battlefields.org/learn/biographies/benjamin-franklin

Portrait of George Washington. (n.d.). American Battlefield Trust. https://www.battlefields.org/learn/biographies/george-washington

Portrait of John Hancock. (n.d.). American Battlefield Trust. https://www.battlefields.org/learn/biographies/john-hancock

Portrait of John Jay. (n.d.). American Battlefield Trust. https://www.battlefields.org/learn/biographies/john-jay

Portrait of John Parker. (n.d.). American Battlefield Trust. https://www.battlefields.org/learn/biographies/john-parker

Portrait of Marquis de Lafayette. (n.d.). American Battlefield Trust. https://www.battlefields.org/learn/biographies/marquis-de-lafayette

Portrait of Sybil Ludington. (n.d.). American Battlefield Trust. https://www.battlefields.org/learn/biographies/sybil-ludington

Portrait of Thomas Jefferson. (n.d.). American Battlefield Trust. https://www.battlefields.org/learn/biographies/thomas-jefferson

Proceedings of the First Continental Congress. (n.d.). USHistory.org. https://www.ushistory.org/declaration/related/congress.html

Ray, R. (2015, August 25). George Washington or John Hanson. Who was the first president? *Journal of the American Revolution.* https://allthingsliberty.com/2015/08/george-washington-or-john-hanson-who-was-the-first-president/

Samuel Adams: Boston's Radical Revolutionary. (2023, January 13). National Park Service. https://www.nps.gov/articles/000/samuel-adams-boston-revolutionary.htm

Saratoga Battle Facts and Summary. (n.d.). American Battlefield Trust. https://www.battlefields.org/learn/revolutionary-war/battles/saratoga

REFERENCES

Siege of Boston, Massachusetts in April 1775 - March 1776. (n.d.). American Revolutionary War. https://revolutionarywar.us/year-1775/siege-of-boston/

Singleton Copley, J. (n.d.). *John Hancock.* Mount Vernon. https://www.-mountvernon.org/library/digitalhistory/digital-encyclopedia/article/john-hancock/

Sons of Liberty American History 1765. (n.d.). Boston Tea Party Ships & Museum. https://www.bostonteapartyship.com/sons-of-liberty

Ten facts about George Washington and the French and Indian War. (n.d.). Mount Vernon. https://www.mountvernon.org/george-washington/french-indian-war/ten-facts-about-george-washington-and-the-french-indian-war/

10 Facts: The Founding Fathers. (2021, July 28). American Battlefield Trust. https://www.battlefields.org/learn/articles/10-facts-founding-fathers#:~:text=Fact%20%231%3A%20These%20seven%20men,most%20as%20the%20Founding%20Fathers

The American Revolution. (n.d.). The American Revolution. https://www.ouramericanrevolution.org/index.cfm/page/view/m0031

The Battle of Bunker Hill June 17, 1775, at Charlestown, Massachusetts. (n.d.). American Revolutionary War. https://revolutionarywar.us/year-1775/battle-bunker-hill/

The colonial experience. (n.d.). USHistory.org. https://www.ushistory.org/gov/2a.asp

13 Colonies Facts | Information, Facts and Worksheets for Kids. (n.d.). KidsKonnect. https://kidskonnect.com/history/13-colonies/#:~:text=Following%20Virginia%2C%20the%20colonies%20of,Georgia%20(1732)%20were%20established

13 Colonies | Facts, information, colonies & history. (2020, February 18). Revolutionary-War.net. https://www.revolutionary-war.net/13-colonies/

Timeline of the Revolution - American Revolution (US). (2022, September 5). National Park Service. https://www.nps.gov/subjects/americanrevolution/timeline.htm

Treaty of Paris (1783). (2022, May 10). National Archives. https://www.archives.gov/milestone-documents/treaty-of-paris

Triber, J.E. (2023, January 13). *Anger and opposition to the Stamp Act (U.S).* National Park Service. https://www.nps.gov/articles/000/anger-and-opposition-to-the-stamp-act.htm

Triber, J.E. (2023, January 13). *Britain Begins Taxing the Colonies: The Sugar & Stamp Acts (U.S).* National Park Service. https://www.nps.gov/articles/000/sugar-and-stamp-acts.htm

Trumbull, J. (n.d.). *Yorktown Campaign.* Mount Vernon. https://www.-mountvernon.org/library/digitalhistory/digital-encyclopedia/article/yorktown-campaign/

Wallenfeldt, J. (2023, July 11). Boston Massacre. Encyclopedia Britannica. https://www.britannica.com/event/Boston-Massacre

Washington's Encampment at Morristown, New Jersey and the "Hard Winter" of 1779-1780. (n.d.). American Battlefield Trust. https://www.battlefields.org/learn/articles/washingtons-encampment-morristown-new-jersey-and-hard-winter-1779-1780#:~:text=The% 20bulk% 20of% 20Washington% 27s% 20Army,Washington% 27s% 20Army% 20to% 20make% 20camp

What was the Olive Branch Petition? (n.d.). Jamestown-Yorktown Foundation. https://www.jyfmuseums.org/learn/research-and-collections/essays/what-was-the-olive-branch-petition#:~:text=The% 20king% 20refused% 20to% 20even,of% 20Rebellion% 20on% 20August% 2023rd

Wheeler, B. (2022, December 15). *The Bill of Rights.* Library of Congress. https://www.loc.gov/item/today-in-history/december-15/#:~:text=On% 20December% 2015% 2C% 201791% 2C% 20the,of% 20peaceful% 20assembly% 20and% 20petition

Who were the original Acton Minutemen? (n.d.). Actonminutemen.org. https://actonminutemen.org/

Who Were the Pilgrims? (n.d.). Plimoth Patuxet Museums. https://plimoth.org/for-students/homework-help/who-were-the-pilgrims

Winter at Valley Forge. (n.d.). American Battlefield Trust. https://www.battlefields.org/learn/articles/winter-valley-forge

Women in the American Revolution. (2017, January 26). American Battlefield Trust. https://www.battlefields.org/learn/articles/women-american-revolution

Zielinski, A.E. (n.d.). *About the Siege of Boston.* American Battlefield Trust. https://www.battlefields.org/learn/articles/siege-boston